SCIENCE OF PRANAYAMA

SCIENCE OF PRANAYAMA

SWAMI SIVANANDA SARASWATI

GYAN

Published by

GYAN

Gyan Publishing House
5, Ansari Road
Daryaganj, New Delhi-110002
Phone: 011-47034999, 9811692060
E-mail: books@gyanbooks.com

Distribution Network
gyanbooks.com
India, USA, Canada, UK, Australia

ISBN: 978-93-6920-661-2 (HB)

First Published, 1941

2nd Impression 2025

Printed at: Gyan Press, Delhi.

SCIENCE OF PRANAYAMA
Author: SWAMI SIVANANDA SARASWATI

SCIENCE OF PRANAYAM

Himalayan Yoga Series

SCIENCE OF PRANAYAM

[REVISED & ENLARGED THIRD EDN.]

BY

SWAMI SIVANANDA SARASWATI

"ANANDA KUTIR," RIKHIKESH (Himalayas)

PULISHERS :

P. K. VINAYAGAM & CO.,

31, Broadway, Madras.

1941

First Edition ... 1935

Second Edition ... 1937

Third Edition ... 1941

THE AUTHOR

ॐ

SANTI SLOKA

हरिः ॐ। वाङ्मे मनसि प्रतिष्ठिता मनो मे
वाचि प्रतिष्ठितमाविरावीर्म एधि वेदस्य म
आणीस्थः श्रुतं मे मा प्रहासीरनेनाधीतेनाहो-
रात्रान्संदधाम्यृतं वदिष्यामि सत्यं वदिष्यामि
तन्मामवतु तद्वक्तारमवत्ववतु मामवतु वक्तारमवतु
वक्तारम्।

ॐ शान्तिः शान्तिः शान्तिः ॥

"Harih Om. My speech is rooted in my mind
My mind is rooted in my speech;
Brahman, reveal thyself to me,
Ye mind and speech enable me
To grasp the truth that the scriptures teach.
Let what I have heard slip not from me;
I join day with night in study,
I think the truth, I speak the truth;
May That protect, may That protect
The teacher, protect me,
Protect the teacher protect the teacher."

Om Peace! Peace!! Peace!!!

ॐ

PARA PUJA

The Highest Worship

O Lord Kesava, what I am thinking of this: How am I to please Thee?

1. The Ganges itself is flowing from Thy feet, shall I take water for Thy ablution then?

2. Thou hast Sat-Chst-Ananda (Absolute Existence, Absolute Consciousness and Absolute Bliss), Swarupa (aspects) as Thy cloth. What Pita (yellow) Pitambara shall I dress Thee with?

3. Thou art dwelling in all creatures (animate and inanimate objects) of the universe, O, Vasudevaj! What Asan shall I give Thee to sit on?

4. Both the Sun and the Moon are serving Thee all through, what is the

use of showing Thee a looking-glass in vain?

5. Thou art the Light of all lights. Now tell me what other light shall I burn for Thee?

6. The Anahat (unceasing eternal sound of "OM") is being continued all day and night to welcome Thee. Shall I then play on drums and cymbals or sound a conch to please Thee?

7. All the four, Vedas, in all the four speeches (sounds) are singing nothing but Thy praise; what hymns shall I sing for Thee then?

8. In all Rasas (flavours) there are but Thy flavour only, what other objects shall I place before Thee, then, as Thy food, Rama?

ॐ

PRAYER

O Antaryamin, Indweller of our hearts! Friend of the poor. Protector of the forsaken! Purifier of the fallen! (*Patitapawan*)! Forgive our sins. Have mercy on us. Show us the easy way, a royal road for attaining the Supreme abode of Peace. Open our inner eye of wisdom (*Jnana-Sakshu or Divya-Drishti*), the eye of intuition as Thou once did for Arjuna, Thy friend and devotee. Throw a flood of light in our Spiritual path. Bless us and lighten the load of our mundane life in this Mrityu-Lokha.

Oh Blessed Lord! All-pervading Truth! Divine effulgence! Remove our hard egoism, lust, wrath, greed, pride, arrogance and Moha (infatuated love for wife, children and property and body or delusion). Cleanse us. Remould us. Make us pure. Give us spiritual strength to attain success in Yoga.

Hari Om Tat Sat.

OM SANTI!

ॐ

INTRODUCTION

To-day for quick travel, the material world presents us the Railway, Steamers, Aeroplanes and so forth, but the Yogis claim that by Yogic culture the weight of the body can be so reduced that it can fly over the space to any distance in an instant. They can prepare a magic ointment, which when applied to the soles of the feet gives them power to traverse any distance on earth within a very short time. By the practice of Khechari Mudra, by applying the elongated tongue to the posterior nasal openings they can fly in the air. By keeping a magic pill in their mouth they can also move in space to any place in the twinkling of an eye. When we are anxious to know how our own relations are doing in a distant or foreign land, we take recourse to writing letters, sending ordinary or urgent cables.

But the Yogis claim that they can by meditation (Dhyana) know anything that happen in other parts of the world by a projection of the mind or by mentally travelling the distance which is only a matter of a few seconds. Yogi Lahiri, whose Samadhi is still in Benares, travelled to London to see the state of health of his superior's wife. For hearing a friend at a long distance the material world presents us with telephones and wireless receivers, but the Yogis claim that through their Yogic power, they can hear anything, from any distance, even the voices of God and other invisible beings in the firmament. To-day when a man is suffering from a disease the material world presents us with doctors, medicines, injections and so forth but the Yogis claim that by a mere glance or by simple touch or by recitation of Mantras not only the disease can be cured but also life can be given to a dead man.

Thus we can see that the Yogis recognised long before this present age that spiritual culture is the most important thing in life and that through this alone anything that can be accomplished in the material sphere, is possible of achievement within a very, very short time. This tendency even in the present day is a dominating factor in Indian life and no one should wonder if he sees people running after Sadhus and Sannyasis, leaving aside the modern scientists in many of their difficulties. Occasionally stories are told of miracles and miraclous powers of ascetics, over the elements of nature or of their remarkable power of curing diseases for which apparently no recognised system of medicine has discovered a drug or a remedy. There are many such Yogis even now in India moving about in jungles, cities, caves and mountains possessing these wonderful, miraculous powers.

These Yogis by persistent effort in concentration get different Yogic powers that are known as "Siddhis." Those who acquire these Siddhis are known as Siddhas. The process through which they obtain Siddhis, is called Sadhan. Pranayam is one of the most important Sadhans. Through the practice of Asans, you can control the physical body and through Pranayam, you can control the subtle, astral body or the Linga Sarir. As there is an intimate connection between the breath and nerve currents, control of breath leads to the control of vital inner currents.

Pranayam occupies a very important place in Indian religion. Every Bramachari and every Grihasti also, has to practise it three times every day, morning, noon and evening in his daily worship during Sandhya. It precedes every religious practice of the Hindus. Before he eats, before he drinks, befere he resolves to do anything, Pranayam should be performed first and then the nature of his determination should be clearly enunciated and placed before the mind. The facts of its preceding every effort of the will is a surety that, that effort will be crowned with success and the mind will be directed to bring about the desired result. Here I may refer to the feat of memory, practised by the Hindu Yogis, under the the name of concentration on one hundred things, "Satavadhana," wherein one hundred questions are put to a Satavadhani or the concentrator in rapid succession by diffreent persons; some testing the verbal memory of the performer; others testing his power of mental caculation; again some others, trying to test his artistic skill, without giving him, any time for comitting the questions to have been put to him, the performer begins, by reproducing the questions, in any order, in respect to those questions with their answers. This is generally done in three or more turns, in each turn giving only a portion of the answer to each of the questions and then continuing from where he left off in the next turn. If the questions are of the nature of mathematical problems whose solutions are required, he delivers, the answers along with the problems, having solved them mentally.

This faculty of concentration of mind is often exhibited not only with reference to the intellect but also with reference to the five senses. A number of bells may be marked differently and the sounds may be allowed to be studied and made mental note of, with the mark given to it. A number of objects of similar shape and colour which are likely to cause deception to the eye of an ordinary man may be shown once to the "Avadhani" with their marks. While he is attending to other things, if a bell were to be struck or one of the objects suddenly exhibited before his sight, he will at once mention the mark of the bell or the number of the object shown. Similary his keenneess of touch is also put to the test. Such feats of memory are not commonly known to any other country. The secret of all this "memory and concentration" of the Hindus may be said to be due to the training which they receive from the daily practice of Pranayam.

The Prana may be defined as the finest vital force in everything which becomes visible on the physical plane as motion and action and on the mental plane as thought. The word Pranayam, therefore, means the restraint of vital energies. It is the control of vital energy which tingles through the nerves of persons. It moves his muscles and causes him to sense the external world and think his internal thought. This energy is of such a nature that it may be called the *vis-viva* of the animal organism. The control of this force is what is aimed at by the Yogis by means of Pranayam. He who conquers this is not only the conqueror of his own existence on the physical and mental plane, but the conqueror of the whole world. For, the Prana is the very essence of cosmic life, that subtle principle, which evolved the whole universe into its present form and which is pushing it towards its ultimate goal. To the Yogi the whole universe is his body. The matter which composes his body is the same that evolved the universe. The force which pulsates through his nerves is not different from the force which vibrates through the universe. The conquest over the body does, therefore, mean to him the conquest over the forces of nature. According to the Hindu Philosophy, the whole nature is composed of two principle substances. One of them is called the Akasa or ether and the other Prana or energy. These two may be said to correspond to mattter and force of the modern scientists. Everything in this universe that possesses form or that has material existence is evolved out of this omnipresent and all-pervasive subtle substance "Akasa." Gas, liquid and solid, the whole universe, consisting of our solar system and millions of huge systems like ours and in fact every kind of existence that may be brought under the world 'created,' are the products of this one subtle and invisible Akasa and at the end of each cycle return to the starting point. In the same way, all the way of forces of nature that are known to man: gravitation, light, heat, electricity, magnetism all those that can be grouped,' under the generic name of 'energy' physical creation, nerve currents, all such as are known as animal forces and thought and other intellectual forces also, may be said to be the manifestations of the cosmic Prana. From Prana, they spring into existence and in Prana, they finally subside. Every kind of force in this universe, physical or mental, can be resolved into this original force. There can be nothing new except these two factors in some one of their forms. Conservation of matter and conservation of energy are the two fundamental laws of nature. While one teaches that the sum-total of Akasa forming the universe is constant, the other teaches that the sum-total of energy that vibrates the universe is also a constant quantity. At the end of each cycle the different manifestations of energy quiet down and become potential: so also the Akasa which becomes indistinguishable: but at the beginning of the next cycle the energies start up again and act on the Akasa so as to involve the various forms. Accordingly when the Akasa changes and becomes gross or subtle, Prana also changes and becomes gross or subtle. As the human body is only a microcosm to a Yogi, his body composed of the nervous system and the internal organs of perception represent to him, the microcosmic Akasa, the nerve currents and thought currents, the cosmic Prana. To understand the secrets of their workings and to control them is, there- get the highest knowledge and the conquest of the universe. Pranayam, in the language of "Yoga" really means the process by which we understand the secret of Prana or vital energies and control them.

He who has grasped this Prana, has grasped the very core of cosmic life and activity. He who has conquered and controlled this very essence, has not only subjected his own body and mind but every other body and mind in this universe. Thus Pranayam or the control of Prana is that means by which the Yogi tries to realise in his little body the whole of cosmic life, and tries to attain perfection by getting all the powers in the universe. His various exercises and trainings are for this one end.

Why delay? Delay means so much additional sufferings and miseries. Let us increase the speed, struggle harder until we succeed in bridging over the vast chasm of time. The aeons of nature may be condensed into the short compass of a life time by the conscious intensification of its thought and action and by proper Sadhan attain this end at once in this body, right now in this very moment? Why not we get that infinite knowledge, infinite bliss, infinite peace and infinite power, now alone?

This solution of the problem is the teaching of Yoga. The whole science 'Yoga' has this one end in view—to enable man to cross the ocean of Samsara, to increase power, to develop knowledge and to develop within one's self the capacity for assimilation.

Om Santi!

"ANANDA KUTIR,"
RIKHIKESH.
1—2—1935.

CONTENTS

CONTENTS—(*contd.*)

CONTENTS—(*contd.*)

CONTENTS—*(contd.)*

CHAPTER I

THE

SCIENCE OF PRANAYAM

CHAPTER I

Prana and Pranayam

Pranayam is an exact Science. It is the fourth Anga or limb of Ashtanga Yoga. "*Tasmin Sati Swasa-praswasa yor-gati-vicchedah pranayamah*—Regulation of breath or the control of Prana is the stoppage of inhalation and exhalation, which follows after securing (that steadiness of posture or seat, Asan)." Thus is Pranayam defined in Patanjali Yoga Sutra Chap. II—49.

Swasa means inspiratory breath and Praswasa is expiratory breath. Breath is external manifestation of Prana, the vital force. Breath, like electricity, is gross Prana. Breath is Sthula, gross. Prana is Sukshma, subtle. By exercising control over this breathing you can control the subtle Prana inside. Control of Prana means control of mind. Mind cannot operate without the help of Prana. The vibrations of Prana only produce thoughts in the mind. It is Prana that moves the mind. It is Prana that sets the mind in motion. It is the Sukshma Prana or psychic Prana that is intimately connected with the mind. Prana is the overcoat for the mind. This breath represents the important fly-wheel of an engine. Just as the other wheels stop when the driver stops the fly-wheel, so also other organs cease working, when the Yogi stops the breath. If you can control the fly-wheel, you can easily control the other wheels. Likewise, if you can control the external breath, you can easily control the inner vital force, Prana. The process by which the Prana is controlled by regulation of external breath is termed Pranayam.

Just as a goldsmith removes the impurities of gold by heating it in the hot furnace, through strongly blowing the blow-pipe, so also the Yogic student removes the impurities of the body and the Indriyas by blowing his lungs *i.e.*, by practising Pranayam.

The chief aim of Pranayam is to unite the Prana with the Apana and take the united Pranapana slowly towards the head. The effect or fruit of Pranayam is Udgata or awakening of the sleeping Kundalini.

What is Prana

"He, who knows Prana knows the Vedas" is the important declaration of the Srutis. You will find in Vedant Sutras: "For the same reason, breath is Brahman." Prana is the sum total of all energy that is manifested in the universe. It is the sum total of all the forces in nature. It is the sum total of all latent forces and powers which are hidden in men and which lie everywhere around us. Heat, light, electricity, magnetism are all the manifestations of Prana. All forces, all powers and Prana spring from the fountain or common source "Atma." All physical forces, all mental forces come under the category 'Prana.' It is force on every plane of being, from the highest to the lowest. Whatever moves or works or has life is but an expression or manifestation of Prana. Akasa or ether also is an expression of Prana. The Prana is related to mind and through mind to will and through will to the individual soul. and through this to the Supreme Being. If you know how to control the little waves of Prana working through the mind, then the secret of subjugating universal Prana will be known to you. The Yogi who becomes an expert in the knowledge of this secret, will have no fear from any power, because he has mastery over all the manifestations of Power in the universe. What is commonly known as Power of personality is nothing more than the natural capacity of a person to wield his Prana. Some persons are more successful in life, more influential and fascinating than others. It is all due to the power of this Prana. Such people manipulate, everyday unconsciously of course, the same influence, which the Yogi uses consciously by the command of his will. There are others, who, by chance, tumble unaware of this Prana and use it for lower purposes under false names. The working of Prana is seen in the systolic and diastolic actions of the heart, when it pumps the blood into the arteries, in the action of inspiration and expiration during the course of breathing; in the digestion of food; in the excretion of urine and faecal matter; in the manufacture of semen, chyle, chyme, gastric juice, bile, intestinal juice, saliva; in closing and opening the eyelids; in walking, playing, running, talking, thinking, reasoning, feeling and willing. Prana is the link between the astral and physical body. When the slender thread-like Prana is cut off, the astral body separates from the physical body. Death takes place. The Prana that was working in the physical body is withdrawn into the astral body.

This Prana remains in a subtle, motionless, unmanifested, undifferentiated state during the cosmic Pralaya. When the vibration is set up, Prana moves and acts upon Akasa, and brings forth the various forms. The macrocosm (Brahmanda) and microcosm (Pinda) are combinations of Prana (energy) and Akasa (matter).

That which moves the steam engine of a train and a steamer; that which makes the aeroplane fly in the air; that which causes the motion of the breath in lungs, that which is the very life of this breath, itself is Prana. I believe, you have now a comprehensive understanding of the term Prana about which you had a very vague conception in the beginning.

By controlling the act of breathing, you can efficiently control all the various motions in the body and the different nerve-currents that are running through the body. You can easily and quickly control and develop body, mind and soul through breath control or the control of Prana. It is through Pranayam that you can control your circumstances and character and can consciously harmonize the individual life with the cosmic life.

The breath, directed by thought under the control of the will, is a vitalising, regenerating force which you can utilise consciously for self-development; for healing many incurable diseases in your system; for healing others and for other various useful purposes.

It is within your easy reach at every moment of your life. Use it judiciously. Many Yogis of yore, like Sri Jnanadev, Trilinga Swami, Ramalinga Swami of Vadalur, and others had utilised this breath, this force, the Prana, in a variety of ways. You can also do so if you practise Pranayam by prescribed breathing exercises. It is Prana that you are breathing rather than the atmospheric air. Inhale slowly and steadily with a concentrated mind. Retain it as long as you can do it comfortably. Then exhale slowly. There should be no strain in any stage of Pranayam. Realise the occult inner life powers which underlie the breath. Become a Yogi and radiate joy, light and power all around you.

Pranavadis or Hatha Yogis consider that Prana Tattwa is superior to Manas Tattwa, the mind principle. They say, Prana is present even when the mind is absent during sleep. Hence Prana plays a more vital part than the mind. If you go through the parables in Kausitiki and Chandogya Upanishads, when all the Indriyas, mind and Prana fight amongst themselves as to their superiority, you will find that Prana is regarded as the highest of all. Prana is the oldest, for it starts its functioning from the very moment the child is conceived. On the contrary the organs of hearing etc., begin to function only when their special abodes *viz.*, the ears, etc., are formed. Prana is called Jeshta, Sreshta (oldest and best) in Upanishads. It is through the vibrations of psychic Prana that the life of the mind, Sankalpa or thinking, is kept up and thought is produced. You see, hear, talk, sense, think, feel, will, know, etc., through the help of Prana and therefore Srutis declare: "Prana is Brahman."

Seat of Prana

The seat of Prana is heart. Though the Antahkarana is one yet it assumes four forms, *viz.*, (i) Manas, (ii) Buddhi, (iii) Chitta and (iv) Ahamkar according to the different functions it performs. Likewise, though the Prana is one, it assumes five forms, *viz.*, (1) Prana, (2) Apana, (3) Samana, (4) Udana and (5) Vyana according to the different functions it performs. This is termed as Tritti Bheda. The principal Prana is called Mukhya Prana. The Prana, joined with Ahamkar, lives in the heart. Of these five, the Prana and the Apana are the chief agents.

The seat of Prana is the heart: of Apana, the anus; of Samana, the region of the naval; of Udana, the throat; while Vyana is all pervading. It moves all over the body.

Sub-Pranas and their Functions

Naga, Kurma, Krikara, Devadatta and Dhananjaya are the five Sub-Pranas.

The function of Prana is respiration; Apana does excretion; Samana performs digestion; Udana does deglutition (swallowing of the food). It takes the Jiva to sleep. It separates the astral body from the physical body at the time of death. Vyana performs circulation of blood.

Naga does eructation and hiccup. Kurma performs the function of opening the eyes. Krikara induces hunger and thirst. Devadatta does yawning. Dhananjaya causes decomposition of the body after death. That man is never re-born, whenever he may die whose breath goes out of the head, after piercing the Brahmarandra.

The Colour of Pranas

Prana is said to be of the colour of blood, red gem or coral. Apana, which is in the middle, is of the colour of Indragopa (an insect of white or red colour). Samana is of the colour between that of pure milk and crystal or of oily and shining colour *i.e.*, of something between both Prana and Apana. Udana is of

Apandara (pale white) colour and that of Vyana, resembles the colour of archil (or that of ray of light).

The Length of the Air Currents

This body of Vayu is 96 digits (6 feet) in length as a standard. The ordinary length of the air current, when exhaled is 12 digits (9 inches). In singing its length becomes 16 digits (1 foot), in eating it comes to 20 digits (15 inches), in sleeping 30 digits (22½ inches; in copulation 36 digits (27 inches) and in doing physical exercise it is much more than that. By decreasing the natural length of the expired air-currents (from 9 inches), life is prolonged and by increasing the current, duration of life is decreased.

The Centering of the Prana

Inhaling the Prana from outside and filling the stomach with it centre the Prana with the mind, in the middle of the navel, at the tip of the nose, and at the toes, during the "Sandhyas" (sunrise and sun-set) or at all times. Thus

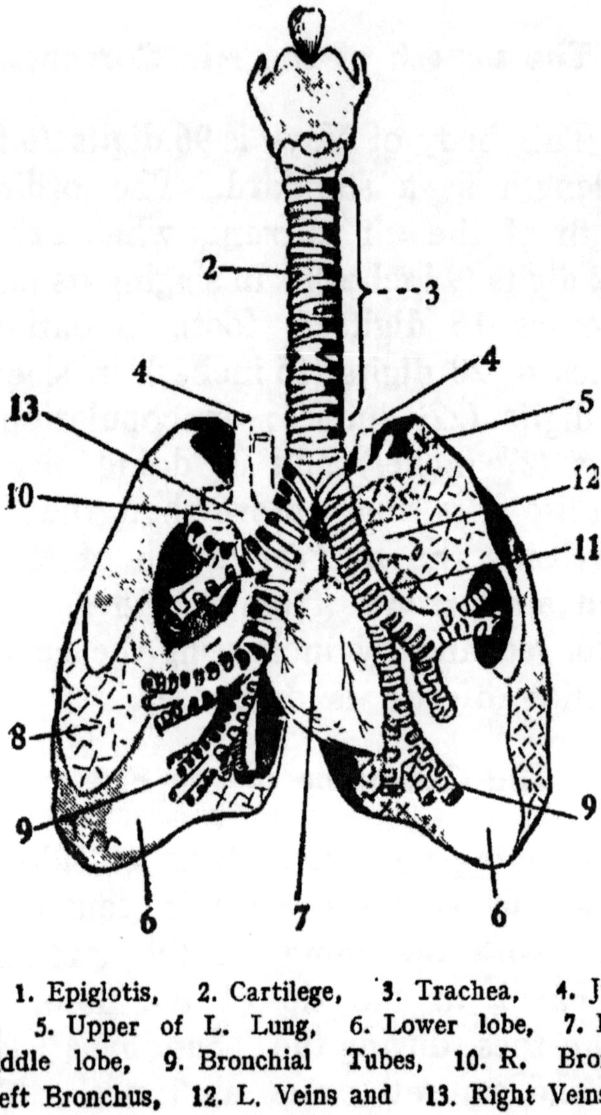

1. Epiglotis, 2. Cartilege, 3. Trachea, 4. Jugular Vein. 5. Upper of L. Lung, 6. Lower lobe, 7. Heart, 8. Middle lobe, 9. Bronchial Tubes, 10. R. Bronchus, 11. Left Bronchus, 12. L. Veins and 13. Right Veins.

the Yogi is freed from all diseases and fatigues. By centering his Prana at the tip of the nose he obtains mastery over the elements of the air; by centering at the middle of his navel all diseases are destroyed; by centering at the toes his body becomes light. He who drinks air through the tongue destroys his fatigue, thirst and many other diseases. For him who drinks the air with his mouth, during the two Sandhyas and the last two hours of the night, within three months, the auspicious Saraswati (Goddess of speech) is present in his Vakh (speech), *i.e.*, he becomes eloquent and learned. In six months he is free from all diseases. Drawing the air at the root of the tongue, the wise man thus drinking nectar enjoys all prosperity.

The Lungs

It will not be out of place here to mention a word on lungs and its functions. The organs of respiration consist of two lungs, one on either side of the chest and the air passages that lead to

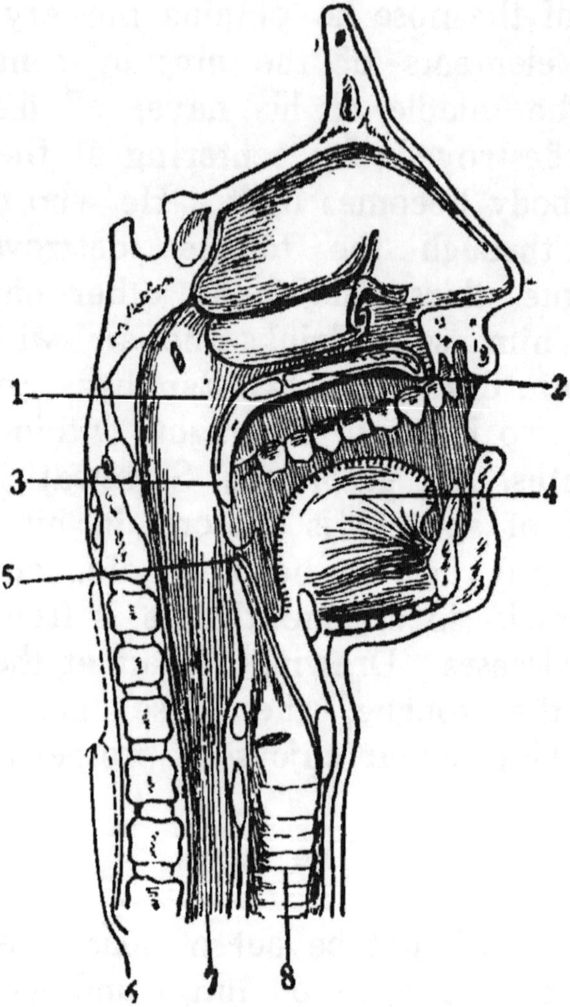

1. Nasal part of Pharynx, 2. Hard palate, 3. Soft palate, 4. Tongue, 5. Epiglotis, 6. Vertebrae, 7. Gullet or Esophagus, 8. Trachea or Larnyx.

them. They are located in the upper thoracic cavity of the chest, one on each side of the median line. They are separated from each other by the heart, the greater blood vessels and the larger air tubes. The lungs are spongy, porous and their tissues are very elastic. The substance of the lungs contains innumerable air-sacs, which contain air. After post-mortem, when it is placed in a basin of water, it floats. They are covered by a delicate serous membrane called the *pleura*, which contains serous fluid to prevent friction of the lungs, during the act of breathing. One wall of the pleura closely adheres to the lung. The other wall is attached to the inner wall of the chest. Through this membrane the lungs are fixed to the wall of the chest. The right lung consists of three lobes. The left lung contains two lobes. Each lung consists of an apex and a base. The base is directed towards the diaphragm, the muscular septum, the dividing wall between upper throat and lower abdomen. The apex is situated above, near the root of the neck. It is the base that gets inflamed in Pneumonia. The apex of the lung, which does not get proper supply of oxygen gets affected by consumption. They afford favourable nidus or breeding ground for Tubercle Bacilli (T. B). By the practice of Kapalabhati and Bhastrika Pranayams and deep breathing exercises these apices get good supply of oxygen and thus phthisis is obviated. Pranayam develops the lungs. He who practises Pranayam will have a powerful, sweet, melodious voice.

The air passages consist of the interior of the nose, pharynx or throat, larynx or the wind box or sounding box, which contain two vocal cords, trachea or windpipe: right and left bronchii and the smaller bronchial tubes. When we breathe, we draw in the air through the nose and after it has passed through the pharynx and larynx, it passes into the trachea or windpipe, thence into the right and left bronchial tubes, which in turn, sub-divide into innumerable smaller tubes called bronchioles, and which terminate in minute subdivisions in the small air-sacs of the lungs, of which the lungs contain millions. The air-sacs of the lungs when spread out over an unbroken surface, would cover an area of 1,40,000 square feet.

The air is drawn into the lungs by the action of the diaphragm. When it expands, the size of the chest and lungs is increased and the outside air rushes into the vacuum thus created. The chest and lungs contract, when diaphragm relaxes and the air is expelled from the lungs.

It is through vocal cords that are located in the larynx that sound is produced. Larynx is the sounding box. When the vocal cords are affected by too much straining as in singing and continuous lecturing, the voice becomes hoarse. In females these cords are shorter. Hence they have a sweet, melodious voice. The number of respiration per minute is 16. In Pneumonia it is increased to 60, 70, 80 per minute. In

Asthma, the bronchial tubes become spasmodic. They contract. Hence there is difficulty in breathing. Pranayam removes the spasm or constriction of these tubes. A small membranous, flat cap covers the upper surface of larynx. It is called Epiglottis. It prevents the food particles or water from entering into the respiratory passage. It acts the part of a safety valve.

When a small particle tries to enter the respiratory passage, cough comes in and the particle is thrown out.

Lungs purify the blood. The blood starts on its arterial journey, bright-red and rich-laden with life giving qualities and properties. It returns by the venous route, poor blue-laden with the waste matter of the system. Arteries are tubes or vessels that carry pure oxygenated blood from the heart towards the different parts of the body. Veins are vessels or tubes that carry back impure blood from the different parts of the body. The right side of the heart contains impure venous blood. From the right side of the heart the impure blood goes to the lungs for purification. It is distributed among the millions of tiny air cells of the lungs. A breath of air is inhalen and the oxygen of the air comes in contact with the impure blood through the thin walls of the hair-like blood vessels of the lungs called pulmonary capillaries. The walls of the capillaries are very thin. They are like muslin cloth or sieve. Blood oozes out or exudes readily. Oxygen penetrates through the walls of these thin capillaries. When the oxygen comes in contact with the tissues, a form of combussion takes place.

The blood takes up oxygen and releases carbonic acid gas, generated from the waste products and poisonous matter, which has been gathered up by the blood from all parts of the system. The purified blood is carried by the four pulmonary veins to the left auricle and thence to the left ventricle. From the ventricle it is pumped into the biggest artery, aorta. From aorta it passes into the different arteries of the body. It is estimated that in a day 35,000 pints of blood traverse the capillaries of the lungs for purification.

From the arteries the pure blood goes into the thin-capillaries. From the capillaries the lymph of the blood exudes, bathes and nourishes the tissues of the body. Tissue respiration takes place in the tissues. Tissues take up the oxygen and leave the carbon-di-oxide. The impurities are taken by the veins to the right side of the heart.

Who is the creator of these delicate structure? Are you feeling the invisible hand of God behind these organs? The structure of this body bespeaks undoubtedly of the omniscience of the Lord. The Antaryamin or the Indweller of our hearts supervises the working of the inner factory as Drishta. Without His presence, heart cannot pump blood into the arteries. Lungs cannot carry out the process of purifying the blood. Pray. Pay your silent homage to Him. Remember Him at all times. Feel His presence in all the cells of the body.

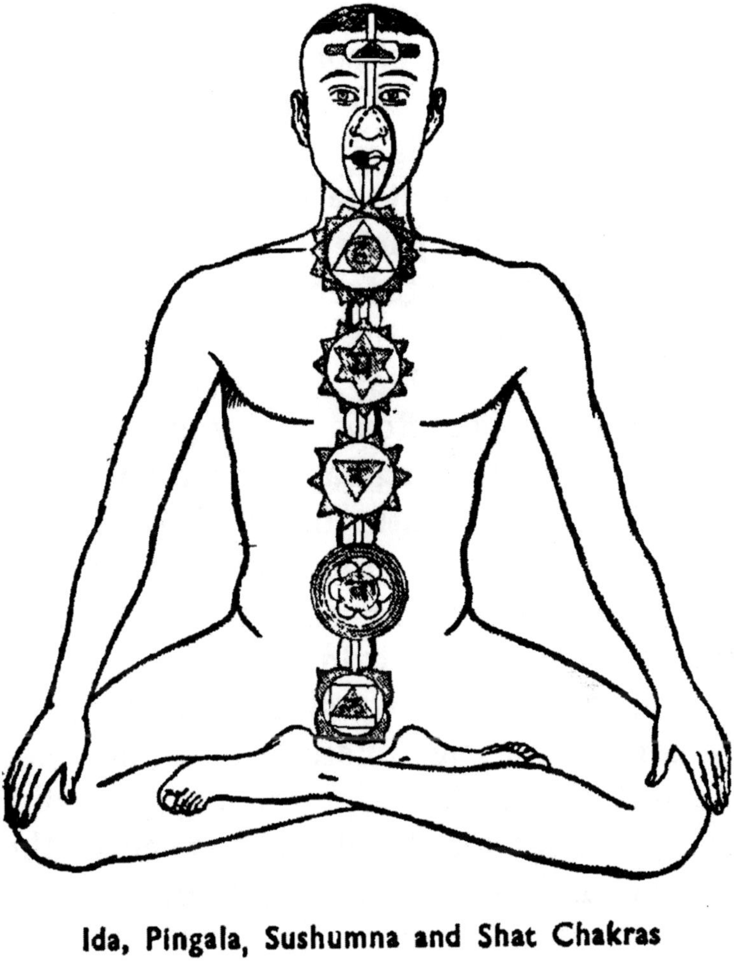

Ida, Pingala, Sushumna and Shat Chakras

Ida and Pingala

There are the two nerve-currents, one on either side of spinal column. The left one is called Ida and the right is known as Pingala. These are Nadis. Tentatively some take these as the right and the left sympathetic cords, but they are subtle tubes that carry Prana. The moon moves in the Ida and the Sun in the Pingala. Ida is cooling. Pingala is heating. Ida flows through the left nostril and the Pingala through the right nostril. The breath flows through the right nostril for one hour and then through the left nostril for one hour. Man is busily engaged in worldly activities, when the breath flows through Ida and Pingala. When Sushumna operates, he becomes dead to the world, he enters into Samadhi. A Yogi tries his level best to make the Prana run in the Sushumna Nadi, which is known as the central Brahmanadi also. On the left of Sushumna is situated Ida and on the right is Pingala. The moon is of the nature of Tamas and the sun is that of the Rajas. The poison share is of the sun and the nectar is of the moon. Ida and Pingala indicate time. Sushumna is the consumer of time.

Sushumna

Sushumna is the most important of all the Nadis. It is the sustainer of the universe and the path of salvation. Situated at the back of the anus, it is attached to the spinal column and extends to the Brahmarandhra of the head and is invisible and subtle. The real work of a Yogi begins when Sushumna begins to function. Sushumna runs along the centre of the spinal cord or spinal column. Above the genital organs and below the navel is the Kanda, of the shape of a bird's egg. There arise from it all the Nadis, 72,000 in number. Of these seventy-two are common and generally known. Of these, the chief ones are ten and they carry the Pranas. Ida, Pingala, Sushumna, Gandhari, Hastijihva, Pusa, Yusasvini, Alambusa, Kuhuh and Sankhini are said to be the ten important Nadis. This Chakra of the Nadis should be known

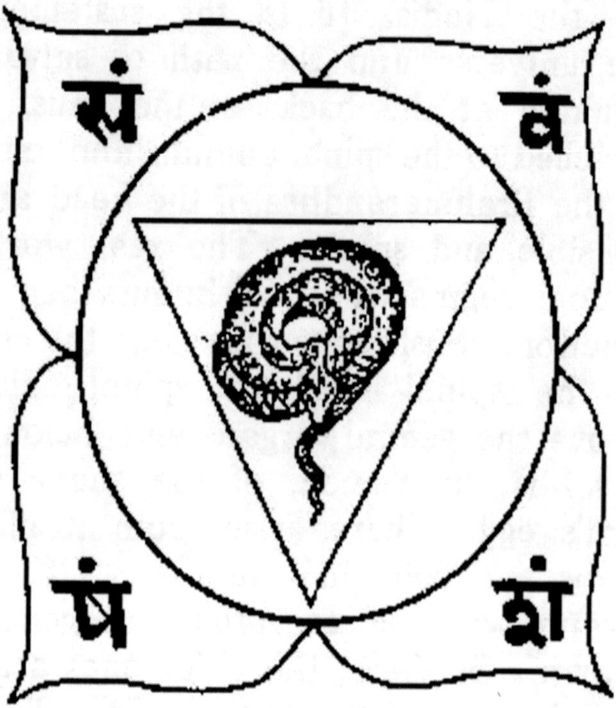

Kundalini and Muladhara Chakra

by the Yogis. Ida, Pingala and Sushumna are said to carry Prana and have Moon, Sun and Agni as their Devatas. When Prana moves in Sushumna, sit for meditation. You will have deep Dhyana. If the coiled up energy, Kundalini, passes up along the Sushumna Nadi and is taken up from Chakra to Chakra, the Yogi gets different sorts of experiences, powers and Ananda.

Kundalini *

Kundalini—is the serpent power or sleeping Shakti, that has 3½ coils with face downwards, in the Muladhara Chakra, at the base of the spine. No Samadhi is possible without its being awakened. The practice of Kumbhak in Pranayam produces heat and thereby Kundalini is awakened and passes upwards along the Sushumna Nadi. The Yogic practitioner experiences various visions. Then the Kundalini passes along the six Chakras and eventually gets united with Lord Siva, seated on the Sahasrara or

* For further particulars see my book, "Kundalini Yoga."

thousand-petalled lotus, at the crown of the head. Nirvikalpa Samadhi ensues now and the Yogi gets liberation and all the divine Aishvaryas. One should practise control of breath with concentration of mind. The awakened Kundalini that is taken up to Manipura Chakra may drop down again to Muladhara. It has to be raised up again with effort. One should become perfectly desireless and should be full of Vairag, before he attempts to awaken Kundalini. Kundalini is like a thread and is resplendent. When it is awakened it hisses like a serpent beaten with a stick and enters the hole of Sushumna. When it travels from Chakra to Chakra, layer after layer of the mind becomes open and the Yogi acquires various Siddhis (psychic powers).

Shat Chakras*

Chakras are centres of spiritual energy. They are located in the astral body, but they have corresponding centres in the physical body also. They

* For a full description refer to "Kundalini Yoga."

can hardly be seen by naked eyes. Only a clairvoyant can see with his astral eyes. Tentatively they correspond to certain plexuses in the physical body. There are six important Chakras. They are:—Muladhara, containing (4 petals) at the anus; Swadhisthana (6 petals) at the genital organ; Manipura (10 petals) at navel; Anahata (12 petals) at the heart; Vishuddha (16 petals at the throat; and Ajna (2 petals) at the space between the two eye-brows. The seventh Chakra is known as Sahasrara, which contains a thousand petals. It is located at the top of the head. Sacral plexus tentatively corresponds to Muladhara Chakra; Protatic plexus to Swadhisthana, Solar plexus to Manipura, Cardiac, plexus to Anahat Chakra, Laryngeal plexus to Vishudda Chakra and Cavernous plexus to Ajna Chakra.

Nadis

Nadis are astral tubes made up of astral matter that carry Pranic currents. They can be seen by the astral eyes only. They are not the nerves. They are

72,000 in number. Ida, Pingala and Sushumna are the important ones. Sushumna is the most important of all.

Purification of Nadis

Pranayam is said to be the union of Prana and Apana. It is of three kinds—expiration, inspiration and cessation. They are associated with the letters of the Sanskrit alphabet for the right performance of Pranayam. Therefore Pranava (ॐ) only is said to be Pranayam. Sitting in Padmasan (Lotus posture) the person should meditate that there is, at the tip of his nose, Devi Gayatri, a girl of red complexion, surrounded by numberless rays of the image of the moon and mounted on Hamsa (Swan), having a mace in her hand. She is the visible symbol of the letter A (अ). The letter U (उ) has as its visible symbol Savitri, a young lady of white colour having a disc in her hand, riding on an eagle (Garuda). The letter M (म) has as its visible symbol Saraswati, an aged woman of black colour, riding on a bull, having a trident in her hand. He should meditate that the single letter, the supreme light—the Pranava OM (ॐ) is the origin or source of these three letters —अ, उ and म. Drawing up the air, through Ida (left nostril) for the space of 16 Matras, he should meditate on the letter A (अ) during that time; retaining the inspired air for the space of 64 Matras he should medidate on the letter U (उ,) during the time; he should then exhale the inspired air for the space of 32 Matras, meditating on the letter M (म) during that time. He should practise thus in the above order again and again.

They having become firm in the posture and having preserved perfect self-control, the Yogi should, in order to clear away the impurities of the Sushumna, sit in Padmasan, and having inhaled the air through the left nostril, should retain it as long as he can and should exhale through the right. Then drawing it again through the right and having retained it, he should exhale it through the left, in the order, that he should draw it through the same nostril, by which he exhaled it before and had retained it. In this context the following verses occur to memory: "In the beginning having inhaled the breath through the left nostril, according to the rule, he should exhale it through the other; then having inhaled the air, through the right nostril, should retain it and exhale it through the other." To those who practise according to these rules, through the right and left nostrils, the Nadis become purified within three months. He should practise cessation of breath at sunrise, at midday, at sunset and at midnight, slowly, till 80 times a day, for 4 weeks. In the early stage, perspiration is produced; in the middle stage the tremour of the body, and in the last stage, levitation in the air. These results ensue out of the repression of the breath, while sitting in the Padma posture, When perspiration arises with effort, one should rub his body well. By this, the body becomes firm and light. In the early course of practice, food with milk and ghee is excellent. One, sticking to this rule, becomes firm in his practice and gets no Tapa (burning sensation) in the body. As lions, elephants and tigers are gradually tamed, so also the breath, when rigidly managed, comes under control.

By the practice of Pranayam, the purification of the Nadis, the brightening of the gastric fire, hearing distinctly of spiritual sounds and good health result. When the nervous centres have become purified through the regular practice of Pranayam the air easily forces its way up through the mouth of the Sushumna, which is in the middle. By the contraction of the muscles of the neck and by the contraction of the one—below *viz.*, Apana, the Prana goes into the Sushumna, which is in the middle, from the west Nadi. Sushumna Nadi is between Ida and Pingala. The Prana which alternates ordinarily between Ida and Pingala, is restrained by long Kumbhak, then along with the soul, its attendant, it will enter the Sushumna, the central Nadi, at one of the three places where it yields space for entrance through such restraint of breath, and in the naval, by the Saraswati Nadi, on the west. After such entry, it is that the Yogi becomes dead to the world, being in that state called Samadhi. Drawing up the Apana and forcing down the Prana from the throat, the Yogi free from old age, becomes a youth of sixteen. Through the practice of Pranayam chronic diseases, that defy Allopathic, Homeopathic, Ayurvedic and Unani doctors, will be rooted out.

When the Nadis have become purified, certain external signs appear on the body of the Yogi. They are lightness of the body, brilliancy in complexion, increase of the gastric fire, leanness of the body, and along with these, the absence of restlessness in the body are all signs of purification.

Shad Karmas

(THE SIX PURIFICATORY PROCESSES)

Those who are of a flabby and phlegmatic constitution only, should practise at first, these six Kriyas, to prepare themselves for the practice of Pranayam, and their success comes in easily. These six Kriyas are: (1) Dhauti, (2) Basti, (3) Neti. (4) Tratak, (5) Nauli and (6) Kapalabhati.

Dhauti

Take a clean piece of Muslin cloth 4 fingers wide and 15 feet long. Dip it in tepid water. The borders of the cloth should be nicely stitched on all sides and no pieces of thread should be hanging loose. Then slowly swallow it and draw it out again. Swallow one foot the first day and increase it daily, little by little. This is called Vastra-dhauti. In the beginning you may have slight retching. It stops on the third day. This practice cures Gulma diseases of the stomach, such as gastritis, dyspepsia, belching, fever, lumbago, asthma, Pleeha (diseases of spleen). leprosy, skin diseases and disorders of phlegm and bile. You need not practise it daily. You can practise it once a week or once in a fortnight. Wash the cloth with soap and keep it always clean. Drink a cup of milk after the practice is over; otherwise you will feel a dry sensation inside.

Basti

This can be practised with or without a bamboo tube. But it is better to have

Utkatasan

a bamboo tube. Sit in a tub of water covering your navel. Assume the posture Utkatasana by resting your body on the forepart of your feet, the heels pressing against the posteriors. Take a small bamboo tube, 6 fingers breadthwise, and insert 4 fingers of its length into the anus after lubricating the tube with vaseline or soap or castor oil. Then contract the anus. Draw the water into the bowels slowly. Shake well the water within the bowels and then expel the water outside. It is known as Jala-Basti. It cures Pleeha, urinary disorders, Gulma, myalgia, dropsy, disorders of digestion, diseases of the spleen and bowels, diseases arising from the excess of wind, bile and phlegm. This Kriya should be done in the morning when the stomach is empty. Drink a cup of milk or take your meals when the Kriya is over. This Kriya can be practised while standing in a river.

There is another way of doing Basti without the help of water. It is called Sthala Basti. Sit in Paschimottanasan on the ground and churn the abdominal and intestinal portions slowly with a downward motion. Contract the sphincter muscles. This removes constipation and all the abdominal disorders. This is not so effective as the Jala Basti.

Neti

Take a thin thread 12 fingers long (½ cubit) without knots. Insert it into the nostrils and passing it inside, draw it out by the mouth. You can also pass the thread through one nostril and pull it through the other. The thread is glued and thereby rendered stiff for passing through easily. This Kriya purifies the skull and produces clear and keen sight. Rhinitis and Coryza are cured thereby.

Tratak—(Gazing)

Gaze steadily without winking with a concentrated mind at any small object, until tears begin to flow. By this practice all diseases of the eye are removed. Unsteadiness of the mind vanishes. Sambhavi Siddhi is obtained. Will power is developed. Clairvoyance is induced.

Nauli

This is abdominal churning with the help of rectus muscle of the abdomen. Bend the head down. Isolate the rectus muscle and turn it from right to left and from left to right. This removes consti-

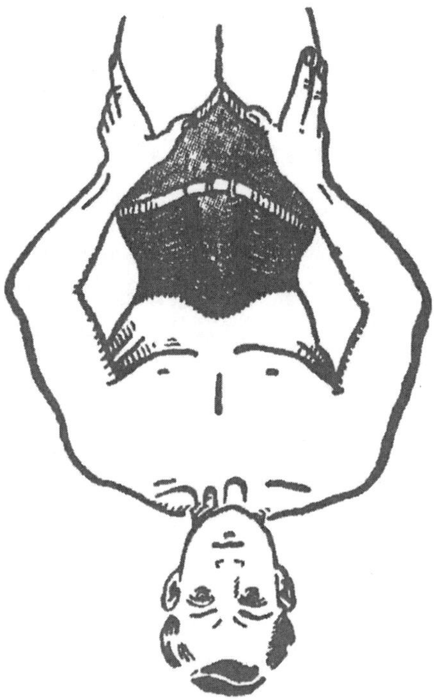

Nauli

pation, increases the digestive fire and destroys all intestinal disorders.

Kapalabhati

Do Rechak and Purak rapidly like the bellows of a black-smith. This destroys all the disorders of phlegm. Detailed instructions are given separately.

CHAPTER II

CHAPTER II

The Meditation Room

Have a separate meditation room under lock and key. Never allow anyone to enter the room. Keep it sacred. If you cannot afford to have a special room for contemplative purposes and for practising Pranayam, have a place in the corner of a quiet room, set apart for this purpose. Have it screened. Place the photo of your Guru or Ishta Devata in the room in front of your Asan. Do Pooja daily for the picture, physically and mentally, before you start meditation and Pranayam. Burn incense in the room or burn Agarbatti (incense sticks). Keep some sacred books there such as Ramayan, Srimad Bhagavatam, Gita, Upanishads, Yoga-Vasishta, etc., for your daily study. Spread a four-folded blanket and over it a piece of soft white cloth. This will serve the purpose of an Asan. Or spread an Asan of Kusa grass. Over it spread a deer or tiger skin. Sit on this

Asan for practising Pranayam and meditation. You can have a raised platform made up of cement. Over this you can spread your Asan. Small insects, ants etc., will not molest you. When you sit on the Asan keep your head, neck and trunk in a straight line. By doing so, the spinal cord that lies with the spinal column will be quite free.

The Five Essentials

Five things are necessary for practising Pranayam. First, a good place; second, a suitable time; third, moderate. substantial, light and nutritious food; fourth, patient and persistent practice with zeal, ease and earnestness and lastly the purification of Nadis (Nadi-Shuddi). When the Nadis are purified the aspirant enters the first stage in the practice of Yoga—"*Arambha.*" A Pranayam practitioner has a good appetite, good digestion, cheerfulness, courage, strength, vigour, a high standard of vitality and a handsome figure. The Yogi should take his food at a time when Surya Nadi or

Pingala is working *i.e.*, when the breath flows through the right nostril, because Pingala is heating and digests the food quickly. Pranayam should not be practised just after taking meals, nor when one is very hungry. Gradually one should be able to retain the breath for 3 Ghatikas (one hour and a half) at a time. Through this, the Yogi gets many psychic powers. When anyone wants to stop the breath for a long period, he should remain by the side of a Yogi Guru, who knows the practice of Pranayam thoroughly. The breath can be suspended by graduated practice from one to three minutes without the help of anybody. Suspension for three minutes is quite sufficient for purifying the Nadis and steadying the mind and for the purpose of good health.

The Place

Select a solitary beautiful and pleasant spot, where there are no disturbances; on the bank of a river, lake or sea or the top of a hill where there is a nice spring and grove of trees, and where milk and articles of food are easily procurable. Build a small Kutir or hut. Have one compound. In the corner of the enclosure, sink a well. It is impossible to get an ideal place that can satisfy you from all view points.

The banks of Narmada, Jumuna, Ganges, Kaveri, Godavari, Krishna are very suitable for building Kutirs or huts. You must select one such spot, where there are some other Yogic practitioners in the neighbourhood. You can consult them in times of difficulties, You will have faith in the Yogic Kriyas. When you see others also who are devoted to such Yogic practices, you will diligently apply yourself in your practice, as you will get an impetus and you will strive to excel them. Nasik, Rikhikesh, Jhansi, Prayag, Uttarkasi, Brindaban, Ayodhya, Benares, etc., are good places. You can fix a spot in a place far from the crowded localities. If you build a Kutir in a crowded place, people out of curiosity will molest you. You will have no spiritual vibrations there. You will be without any protection if you build your cottage in a thick forest. Thieves and wild animals will trouble you. The question of difficulty for food will arise. In Swetaswatara Upanishad it is said: "At a level place, free from pebbles, fire and gravel; pleasant to the eyes, and repairing to a cave, protected from the wind, let a person apply his mind to God."

Those who practise in their own houses can convert a room into a forest. Any solitary room will serve their purpose well.

The Time

The practice of Pranayam should be commenced in Vasanta Ritu (spring) or Sarat Ritu (autumn). Because in these seasons success is attained without any difficulty or trouble. The Vasanta is the period during March and April. The Sarat, autumn last during September and October. In summer do not practise Pranayam, in the afternoon or evening. In the cool morning hours you can have your practice.

The Adhikari (the Qualified Person)

One who has a calm mind, one who has subdued his Indriyas, one who has faith in the words of the Guru and Shastras, one who is an Astika (*i.e.*, one who believes in God) and one who is moderate in eating, drinking and sleeping and one who has an eager longing for deliverance from the wheel of births and deaths—is a qualified person for the practice of Yoga. Such a man can easily get success in the practice of Pranayam or any other Yogic practice. Pranayam should be practised with care, perseverance and faith.

Those who are addicted to sensual pleasures or those who are arrogant dishonest, untruthful, diplomatic, cunning and treacherous; those who disrespect Sadhus, Sannyasins and their Gurus or spiritual preceptors, and take pleasure in vain controversies, or of a highly talkative nature, those who are disbelievers, mix much with worldly-minded people, are cruel, harsh and greedy and do much useless Vyavahara, can never attain success in Pranayam or any other Yogic practices.

There are three types of Adhikaries—*viz.*, (1) good (Uttama), (2) middle (Madhyama) and (3) inferior (Adhama) according to Samskaras, intelligence, degree of Vairag, Vivek and Mumukshatwa and the capacity for Sadhan.

You must approach a Guru, who knows Yogashastra and have mastery over it. Sit at his lotus feet. Serve him. Clear your doubts through sensible and reasonable questions. Receive instructions and practise them with proper enthusiasm, zeal, attention, earnestness and faith, according to the methods taught by the teacher.

A Pranayam practitioner should always speak kind and sweet words. He must be kind to everybody. He must love all. He must be honest. He must speak the truth. He must develop Vairag, patience, Sraddha (faith), Bhakti (devotion), Karuna (mercy), etc. He must observe perfect celibacy. A householder should be very moderate in sexual matters during the practice.

Dietetic Discipline

The proficient in Yoga should abandon articles of food, detrimental to the practice of Yoga. He should give up salt, mustard, sour, hot, pungent and bitter things, asafoetida, worship of fire, women, too much walking, bathing at sun-rise, emaciation of the body by fasts, etc. During the early stages of practice, food of milk and ghee is ordained; also food consisting of wheat, green pulse and red rice is said to favour the progress. Then he will be able to retain his breath as long as he likes. By thus retaining the breath as long as he likes, Kevala Kumbhak (cessation of breath without inspiration and expiration) is attained. When Kevala Kumbhak is attained by one, expiration and inspiration are dispensed with. There is nothing unattainable in three worlds for him. In the commencement of his practice, sweat is getting out. As a frog moves by leaps, so the Yogi sitting in Padmasan moves on the earth. With a further increased practice, he is able to rise from the ground. He, while seated in lotus posture levitates. Then arises in him the power to perform extraordinary feats. Any pain, small or great, does not affect the Yogi. Then excretions and sleep are diminished; tears, rheum in the eye, salivary flow, sweat and bad smell in the mouth, do not arise in him. With a still further practice, he acquires great strength by which he attains Bhuchara Siddhi, which enables him to bring under his control all the creatures that tread on this earth; tigers, Sarabhas, elephants, wild bulls and lions even die by a blow given by the palm of this Yogi. He becomes as beautiful as the God of Love himself. By the preservation of the semen a good odour pervades the body of the Yogi.

Yogic Diet

Instinct or voice within will guide you in the selection of articles of diet. You are yourself the best judge to form a Sattwic Yogic menu to suit your temperament and constitution. Further information is given in the "Appendix."

Mitahara

Take wholesome Sattwic food half stomachful. Fill a quarter with pure water. Allow the remaining quarter free for expansion of gas and for propitiating the Lord.

Purity in Food

"*Ahara Suddhau Sattwa Suddhih, Sattwa Suddhau Dharma Smriti, Smriti tabhe sarvagranthinam viprana mokshah.*"

By the purity of food, follows the purification of the inner nature, on the purity of the inner nature, the memory becomes firm and on the strengthening of memory follows the loosening of all ties, and the wise get liberation thereby.

You must not practise Pranayam just after meals. When you are very hungry, then also you must not practise. Go to the water closet (W.C.) and empty the bowels before you begin Pranayam. A Pranayam practitioner should observe Samyama (control) in food and drink.

Those who are strict and regular in diet derive immense benefits during the course of practice. They get success quickly. Those persons who suffer from chronic constipation and who are in the habit of defaecating in the afternoon can practise Pranayam in the early morning without answering the calls of nature. They should try their level best by some means or other to get an evacuation of their bowels in the early morning.

Food plays a very important role in Yoga Sadhan. An aspirant should be very, very careful in the selection of article of diet of Sattwic nature, in the beginning of his Sadhan period. Later on when Pranayam Siddhi is obtained, drastic dietic restrictions can be removed.

Charu

This is a mixture of boiled, white rice, ghee, sugar and milk. This is a wholesome combination for Brahmacharis and Pranayam practitioners.

Milk Diet

Milk should be scalded but not too much boiled. The process of scalding is that the milk should be immediately removed from the fire, as soon as the boiling point is reached. Too much boiling destroys the Vitamin, the mysterious nutritive principles and renders it quite useless as an article of diet. Milk is a perfect food by itself, containing as it does, the different nutritive constituents in a well-balanced proportion. It leaves very little residue in the bowels. This is an ideal food for Yogic students during Pranayam practice.

Fruit Diet

A fruit diet exercises a benign, soothing influence on the constitution and is a very desirable diet for Yogis. This is a natural form of diet. Fruits are very great energy producers. Bananas, grapes, sweet oranges, apples, pomegranates, mangoes, *Chikkus* (Sappota), and dates are wholesome fruits. Lemons possess anti-scorbutic properties and act as restoratives to blood. Fruit juice contains vitamin C. *Chikkus* increase pure blood. Mangoes and milk—is a healthy agreeable combination. You can live on mangoes and milk alone. Pomegranate juice is cooling and is very nutritious Bananas are very nutritious and substantial. Fruits help concentration and easy mental focussing.

Articles allowed

Barley, wheat, ghee, milk, almonds promote longevity and increase power and strength. Barley is a fine article of diet for a Yogi and Sadhak. It is cooling too. Sri Swami Narayan, the author of "Ek Sant ka Anubhav," who wears a Kowpeen of gunny bag, lives on bread made up of barley. He recommends barley bread to his disciples. It is said that Emperor Akbar lived upon barley.

You can take wheat, rice, barley, milk, bread, cow's milk, ghee, sugar, butter, sugar candy, honey, dried ginger

(Sonte), green pulse, *Moong dal*, *Pancha-shaka* vegetables, *Pey-pudalai*, potatoes, resins, dates, light Khichdi of green dal. Khichdi is a light food and it can be agreeably taken. The food should be reduced in proportion to the increase in Kumbhak. You must not reduce your food much, in the beginning of your practice. You must use your common-sense, all throughout the Sadhan. *Toorki dal* can be taken. The *Pancha-shaka* belong to the species of spinach. They are excellent vegetables, the thick succulent young leaves are boiled and seasoned or fried with ghee. They are five in number, *viz.,—Seendil*, *Chakravarthi*, *Ponnangani*, *Chirukeerai* and *Vellai-charnai keerai*. When the Pingala or Suryanadi runs in the right nostril, you must take your food. Suryanadi produces heat. It will digest the food well. You may take jack-fruit, cucumber, brinjal, plantain stem, *Laukee*, *Parwal* and *Bhendi* (lady's finger).

Articles Forbidden

Highly seasoned dishes, hot curries, chutnies, meat, fishes, chillies, sour articles, tamarind, mustard, all kinds of oil, asafoetida, salt, garlic, onions, *Urdukidal*, (black gram), all bitter things, dry foods, black sugar, vinegar, alcohol, sour curd, stale foods, acids, astringents, pungent stuff, roasted things, heavy vegetables, over-ripe or unripe fruits, pumpkins, etc., must be avoided. Meat can make man a scientist but rarely a Philosopher, Yogi or a Tattwa Jnani. Onions and garlic are worse than meat. All food-stuffs contain a small quantity of salt. So, even if you do not add salt separately, the system will derive the necessary quantity of salt from other food-stuffs. The giving up of salt will not produce deficiency of hydrochloric acid and dyspepsia as allopathic doctors foolishly imagine. Salt excites passions. No ill-effects are produced by the giving up of salt. Mahatma Gandhi and Swami Yoganandaji of Lucknow have given up salt for over thirteen years. Giving up salt helps you in controlling the tongue and thereby the mind also and in developing will power too. You will have good health. Sitting before fire, fasting company of women and worldly-minded people, Yatra, long walk, carrying heavy burdens, cold bath in the early morning, harsh words, speaking untruth, dishonest practices, theft, killing animals, Himsa of all kinds either in thought, word or deed, hatred and enmity towards any person, fighting, quarreling, pride, double-dealing, intriguing, back-biting, tale-bearing, crookedness, talks of other than those of Atma and Moksha, cruelty towards animals and men, too much fasting or eating only once every day, etc., are not allowed for a Pranayam practitioner.

A Kutir for Sadhan

The Pranayam student should erect a beautiful monastery with a very small opening and with no crevices. It should be well pasted with cow dung or with white cement. It should be absolutely free from bugs, mosquitoes and lice. It should be swept well every day, with a broom. It should be perfumed with good odour and fragrant resins should be burnt therein. Having taken his seat, neither too high nor too low, on an Asan, made of a cloth, deer skin and Kusha grass, one over the other, a wise man should assume the lotus posture and keeping his body erect and his hands folded in respect should salute his tutelary deity and Sri Ganesh by repeating "*Om Sri Ganeshaya Namah.*" Then he should begin to practise the Pranayam.

Matra

The time taken in making a round of the knee with the palm of the hand, neither very slowly nor quickly and snapping the fingers once, is called a Matra.

Each time-unit is called a Matra. The twinkling of an eye is sometimes taken as the period of one Matra. Time occupied by one normal respiration is considered as one Matra. Time taken up in pronouncing the mono-syllable, OM, is regarded as one Matra. This is very convenient. Many Pranayam practitioners adopt this time-unit in their practice.

Padmasan

This also known by the name Kamalasan. Kamala means lotus. When the Asan is demonstrated it presents the appearance of a lotus in a way. Hence the name Padmasan.

Padmasan

(LOTUS POSE)

Amongst the four poses prescribed for Japa and Dhyana, Padmasan comes foremost. It is the best Asan for contemplation. Rishis like Gheranda, Sandilya speak very highly of this vital Asan. This is highly agreeable for house-holders. Even ladies can sit in this Asan. Padmasan is suitable for lean persons and for youths as well.

TECHNIQUE

Sit on the ground by spreading the legs forward. Then place the right foot on the left thigh and the left foot on the right thigh. Place the hands on the knee joints. You can make a finger-lock and keep the locked hands over the left ankle. This is very convenient for some persons. Or you can place the left hand over the left knee and the right hand over the right knee with the palm facing upwards and the index finger touching the middle portion of the thumb (Chin Mudra).

Siddhasan

(The Perfect Pose)

Next to Padmasan comes Siddhasan in importance. Some eulogize this Asan as even superior to Padmasan for purposes of Dhyana (contemplation). If you get mastery over this Asan, you will acquire many Siddhis. Further it was being practised by many Siddhas (perfected Yogis) of yore. Hence the name Siddhasan.

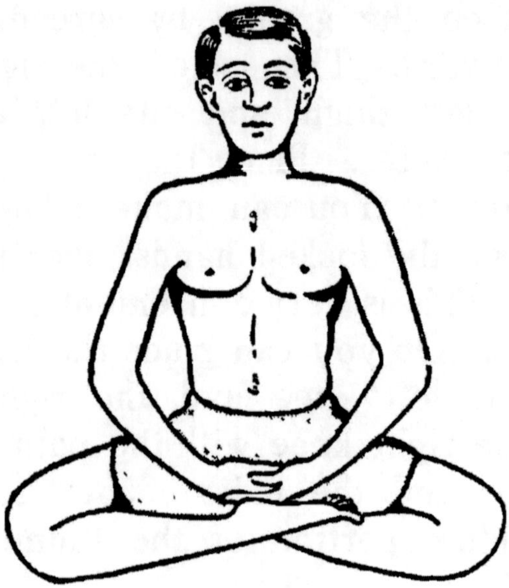

Siddhasan

(THE PERFECT POSE)

Even fatty persons with big thighs can practise this Asan easily. In fact this is better to some persons than Padmasan. Young Brahmacharis, who attempt to get established in celibacy, should practise this Asan. This is not suitable for ladies.

TECHNIQUE

Place the left heel at the anus or Gudha, the terminal opening of the alimentary canal or digestive tube. Keep the right heel on the root of the generative organ. The feet or legs should be so nicely arranged that the ankle joints should touch each other. Hands can be placed as in Padmasan.

Swastikasan

(Prosperous Pose)

Swastika is sitting at ease with the body erect. Spread the legs forward. Fold the left leg and place the feet near the right thigh muscles. Similarly bend the right leg and push the feet in the space between the thigh and calf muscles. Now you will find the two feet between the thighs and calves of the legs. This is very comfortable for meditation. Keep the hands as instructed in Padmasan.

Samasan

Place the left heel at the beginning of right thigh and the right heel at the

Samasan

(EQUAL POSE)

beginning of left thigh. Sit at ease. Do not bend either on the left or right. This is called as Samasana.

Three Bandhas

There are four Bhedas (piercings or division) *viz.*, Surya, Ujjayee, Sitali and

Basti. Through these four ways, when Kumbhak is near or about to be performed, the sinless Yogi should practise the three Bandhas. The first is called Mula Bandha. The second is called Uddiyana, and the third is Jalandhara. Their nature

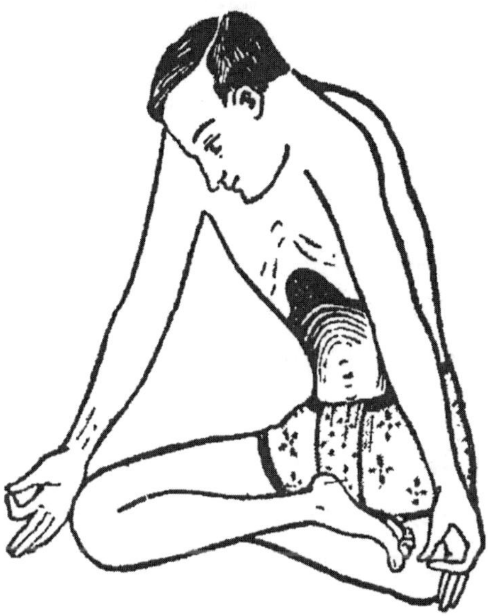

Bandha Traya

will be thus described. Apana which has a downward tendency is forced up by bending down. This process is called Mula Bandha. When Apana is raised up and reaches the sphere of Agni (fire), then the flame of Agni grows long, being blown about by Vayu. The Agni and Apana come to or commingle with Prana in a heated state. Through this Agni, which is very fiery, arises in the body the flaming or the fire which rouses the sleeping Kundalini makes a hissing noise, becomes erect like a serpent beaten with a stick and enters into the hole of Brahmanadi (Sushumna). Therefore Yogis should daily practise Mula Bandha. Uddiyana should be performed at the end of Kumbhak and at the beginning of expiration. Because Prana '*Uddiyate*'—goes up the Sushumna in this Bandha, it is called Uddiyana by the Yogis. Being seated in the Vajra posture and holding firmly the two toes by the two hands near the two ankles, he should gradually upbear the Tana (thread or Nadi, the Saraswati Nadi) which is on the western side of Udara (the upper part of the abdomen, (above the navel), then to the heart and then to the neck. When Prana reaches the Sandhi (junction) of navel, slowly it removes the diseases of the navel. Therefore this should be practised perfectly.

The Bandha called Jalandhara should be practised at the end of Purak. This

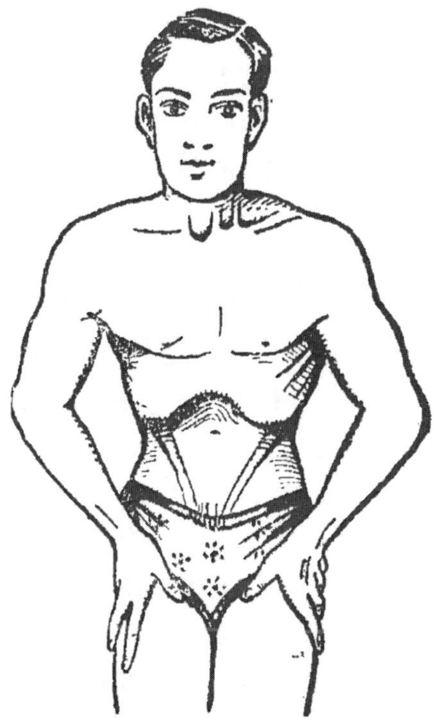

Uddiyana in standing

Jalandhara is of the form of the contraction of the neck and is an impediment to the passage of Vayu upwards. When the neck is contracted by bending the head downwards, so that the chin may touch the chest, Prana goes through Brahma-nadi. Assuming the seat, as mentioned before, one should stir up Saraswati and control Prana. On the first day Kumbhak should be done four times, on the second day ten times and then five times separately. On the third day twenty times will do and afterwards Kumbhak should be performed with the Bandhas and with an increase of two times per day.

Arambha Avastha

Pranava (ॐ) should be chanted with three Matras (prolonged intonations). This is for the destruction of the former sins. The Mantra Pranava destroys all obstacles and all sins. By practising this he attains the 'Arambha Avastha' (the beginning or first stage). The body of the Yogi begins to perspire. When it perspires, he should rub it well with the hands. The trembling of the body also occurs. He sometimes jumps like a frog.

Ghata Avastha

Then follows the Ghata Avastha, the second state, which is acquired by constantly practising suppression of breath. When a perfect union takes place between Prana and Apana, Manas and Buddhi or Jivatma and Paramatma without opposition, it is called the Ghata Avastha. He may now practise only for about one fourth of the period prescribed for practice before. By day and by evening let him practise only for a Yama (3 hours). Let him practise the (Kevala Kumbhak once a day. Drawing away completely the organs from the objects of senses during cessation of breath is called Pratyahara. Whatever he sees with his eyes, let him consider as Atma. Whatever he hears with his ears, let him consider as Atma. Whatever he smells with his nose, let him consider as Atma. Whatever he tastes with his tongue, let him consider as Atma. Whatever the Yogi touches with his skin, let him consider as Atma. Then various wonderful powers are obtained by the Yogi, such as clairvoyance, clairaudience, ability to transport himself to great distances within a moment, great power of speech, ability to take up any form he likes, ability to become invisible and the wonder of transmuting iron into gold, when the former is smeared with his excretion.

That Yogi, who is carefully practising Yoga, attains the power to levitate. Then should the wise Yogi think that these powers are great obstacles in the attainment of Yoga. And so he should never take delight or recourse to them. The Yogis should not exercise these powers before any person whatsoever. He should live in the world as a fool or an idiot or as a deaf man in order to keep his powers concealed. His disciples would without doubt request him to show them his powers for the gratification of their desire. One, who is actively engaged in one's (world-imposed) duties, forgets to practise Yoga. So he should practise day and night nothing but Yoga without forgetting the words of his Guru. Thus he who is constantly engaged in Yogic practices, passes the Ghata-state. Nothing is gained by useless company (of worldly-minded people). Therefore one should with great effort shun evil company and practise Yoga.

Parichaya Avastha

Then by such constant practice the Parichaya Avastha (the third state) is gained. Vayu or breath, through arduous practice pierces the Kundalini, along with Agni through thought and enters the Sushumna, uninterrupted. When one's Chitta enters Sushumna along with Prana, it reaches the high seat in the head, along with Prana. When the Yogi by the practice of Yoga acquires power of action (Kriya Shakti) and pierces through the six Chakras and reaches the secure condition of Parichaya, the Yogi then verily sees the three-fold effects of Karma. Then let the Yogi destroy the multitude of Karmas by the Pranava (ॐ). Let him accomplish "Kaya-Vyuha," a mystical process of arranging the various Skandas of the body and taking various bodies, in order to exhaust all his previous Karmas without the necessity of being reborn. At that time let the great

Yogi practise the *five-fold *Dharanas* or forms of concentration by which command over five elements is gained and fear of injuries by any one of them is removed.

Nishpatti Avastha

This is the fourth stage of Pranayam. Through graduated practice the Yogi reaches the Nishpatti Avastha, the state of consummation. The Yogi, having destroyed all the seeds of Karma, drinks the nectar of immortality. He feels neither hunger nor thirst, nor sleep nor swoon. He becomes absolutely independent. He can move anywhere in the world. He is never reborn. He is free from all diseases, decay and old age. He enjoys the bliss of Samadhi. He is no longer in need of any Yogic practice. When the skilful tranquil Yogi can drink the Prana Vayu by placing the tongue at the root of the palate, when he knows the laws of action of Prana and Apana, then he becomes entitled to liberation.

---

*Described in the "*Appendix.*"

A Yogic student will automatically experience all these Avasthas one by one as he advances in his systematic, regular practices. An impatient student cannot experience any of these Avasthas through occasional practices. Care should be taken in the observances of Mithahara and Brahmacharya.

CHAPTER III

CHAPTER III

What is Pranayam ?

Tasmin Sati Swasa praswasayorgati vicchedah Pranayamah—"Regulation of breath or the control of Prana is the stoppage of inhalation and exhalation, which follows after securing that steadiness of posture or seat."

This is the definition of Pranayam in Patanjali Yoga Sutras Chapt. II Sutra 49.

'Swasa' means inspiratory breath. Praswasa means expiratory breath. You can take up the practice of Pranayam after you have gained steadiness in your Asan (seat). If you can sit for 3 hours in one Asan, continuously at one stretch, you have gained mastery over the Asan. If you are able to sit from half to one hour even, you can take up the practice of Pranayam. You can hardly make any spiritual progress without the practice of Pranayam.

Prana is Vyashti, when the individual is concerned. The sum total of the cosmic energy or cosmic Prana is Hiranyagarbha who is known as the floating 'Golden Egg." Hiranyagarbha is Samashti Prana. One match stick is Vyashti (single). The whole match box is Samashti. A single mango-tree is Vyashti. The whole mango grove is Samashti. The energy in the body is Prana. By controlling the motion of the lungs or respiratory organs, we can control the Prana that is vibrating inside. By control of Prana, the mind can be easily controlled, because the mind is fastened to the Prana, like the bird to the string. Just as the bird that is tied to a post by a string, after flying here and there finds its resting place to the post, so also this mind-bird after running hither and thither in various sensual objects finds its resting place during deep slumber in the Prana.

Pranayam

(According to the Gita)

Apana Juhvati Pranam Pranapana tatapare

Pranapanagatih ruddhwa Pranayama parayanah.

Gita Ch. IV—29.

Others offer Prana (outgoing breath) in Apana (incoming breath) and Apana in Prana, restraining the passage of Prana and Apana, absorbed in Pranayam. Pranayam is a precious Yajna (sacrifice). Some practise the kind of Pranayam called Purak (filling in). Some practise the kind of Pranayam called Rechak (emptying). Some are engaged in the practice of Pranayam called Kumbhak, by impeding the outward passage of air, through the nostrils and the mouth, and by impeding the inward passage of the air, in the opposite direction.

Pranayam

(According to Sri Sankaracharya)

"Pranayam is the control of all life-forces by realising naught but Brahman in all things as the mind, etc."

"The negation of the Universe is the out-going breath. The thought: "I am Brahman" itself is called the incoming breath."

"The permanence of that thought thereafter is the restrained breath. This is the Pranayam of the wise, while the pressing of the nose is only for the unknowing."

[*Aparokshanubhuti* 118—120].

Pranayam

(According to Yogi Bhusunda)

Bhusunda says to Sri Vasishta:—"In the cool lotus of the heart within this visible tenement of flesh composed of the five elements, there are two Vayus, *viz.*, Prana and Apana, commingled in it. Those who tread smoothly and without any of the slightest efforts, the path of these two Vayus will become the sun and the moon themselves in the heart-Akasa and will rove in the Akasa and yet be animating and carrying their fleshy tabernacle. These Vayus will go up and down to higher and lower states. They are of the same nature in the waking dreaming and dreamless-sleeping states, and permeate all throughout. I am moving in the direction of these two

Vayus and have rendered nil all my Vasanas in the waking states like unto those of the dreamless sleeping state. Divide a filament of the lotus stalk into a thousand times and you will find these Vayus more subtle than that. Hence it is difficult for me to treat about the nature of these Vayus and their vibrations. Of these, Prana does ceaselessly vibrate in this body with an upward motion, both externally and internally, while Apana having the same fluctuating tendency, vibrates both external and internal to the body having a downward motion. It will be beneficial if the Prana exhaled to the extent of 16 digits is inhaled to the same extent. Only 12 digits are inhaled ordinarily. Those who have brought to experience—*viz.*, the equalisation of Prana in exhalation and inhalation will enjoy infinite bliss.

"Now hear about the characteristics of Prana. The inhalation to the length of 12 digits of the Prana, which has been exhaled is called (the internal) Purak (inhalation). This also is called the internal (Purak), when Apana Vayu re-enters the body from outside without any effort. When Apana Vayu ceases to manifest itself and Prana gets absorbed in the heart, then the time occupied in such a state is (the internal) Kumbhak. Yogis are able to experience all these. When the Prana in the Akasa of the heart manifests itself externally (to the heart within) in diverse aspects without any affliction to the mind, then it is called (the external) Rechak (exhalation). When the externally fluctuating Prana enters the nose and stops there at its tip, then it is called the external Purak. But when it is passing from the tip of the nose, it goes down 12 digits. Then also it is called the external Purak. When Prana goes arrested without and Apana within, then it is called the external Kumbhak. When the shining Apana Vayu takes an upward bent within, then it is styled the external Rechak. All these practices lead to Moksha. Therefore they should ever be meditated upon. Those who have understood and practised well all the external and internal Kumbhaks and others, will never be reborn.

"All the eight courses, I have given out before, are capable of yielding Moksha. They should be practised both day and night. Those who are associated with these practices smoothly and control their minds, by not letting them run in other directions, will, in course of time attain Nirvana. Such practitioner will never thirst after material pleasures, They will ever be in their uniform practice, whether walking or standing, waking, dreaming or sleeping.

"Prana, having flown out, will again be absorbed in the heart having run back 12 digits. Similarly will Apana be absorbed in the heart, having issued out of the heart and running back 12 digits to it. Apana being the moon, will cool the whole body in its passage. But Prana being the sun, will generate heat in the system and cook or digest everything in it. Will pains arise in one who has reached that supreme state, where the Kalas (rays) of Apana, the moon, are drowned by Prana, the sun? Will rebirth arise in one who has reached that powerful seat, when the Kalas of Prana, the sun, are devoured by Apana, the moon? Those will arrest at once the seven births who reach that neutral state, where they find Apana Vayu consumed by Prana and *vice versa.* I eulogise that Chidatma, who is in that intermediate state, where Prana and Apana are absorbed in one another. I meditate ceaselessly upon that Chidatma, who is in the Akasa, directly in front, at the end of my nose, where Prana and Apana both become extinct. Thus it is through this path of Prana's control, that I attained the supreme and immaculate Tattwa, devoid of pains."

Control of Breath

The first important step is to master the Asan or the posture or to control the body. The next exercise is Pranayama. *Correct posture is indispensably* requisite for the successful practice of Pranayama. Any easy comfortable posture is Asan. That pose is the best which continues to be comfortable for the greatest length of time. Chest, neck and head must be in one vertical line. You should not bend the body either forwards or laterally *i.e.*, either on the right or left side. You should not sit crooked. You should not allow the body to collapse. You must not bend the body either forwards or backwards. By regular practice the mastery over the pose will come by itself. Fatty people will find it difficult to practise the Padma Asan or the Lotus Pose. They can sit on the comfortable pose (Sukha Asan) or Siddha Asan (perfected pose). You need not wait for practising Pranayama till you get full mastery over the Asan. Practise Asan and side by side you can practise Pranayama also. In course of time you will acquire perfection in both. Pranayama can be practised by sitting in the chair also by sitting erect.

In Bhagavat Gita, the Immortal Song of Lord Krishna you will find a beautiful description of seat and pose. In a pure secret place by himself established in a fixed seat of his own, neither too high nor too low, with cloth, black antelope skin and Kusa grass, one over the other, there, making the mind one-pointed, with thought and the functions of the senses controlled, steady on his seat, he should practise Yoga for the purification of the Self, holding the body, head and neck erect, firm, gazing steadily at the tip of the nose without looking around. (Chapter VI—10, 11 and 12).

Pranayama is the control of the Prana and the vital forces of the body. It is regulation of the breath. This is the most important step. The aim of Pranayama is the control of Prana. Pranayama begins with the regulation of the breath for having control over the life-currents or inner vital forces. In other words Pranayama is the perfect control of the life-currents through control of breath. Breath is external manifestation of the gross Prana. A correct habit of breathing must be established by the regular practice of Pranayama. In ordinary worldly persons the breathing is irregular.

If you can control the Prana you can completely control all the forces of the Universe, mental and physical. The Yogi can also control the Omnipresent manifesting power out of which all energies take their origin, whether concerning magnetism, electricity, gravitation, cohesion, nerve currents, vital forces or thought vibrations, in fact the total forces of the Universe, physical and mental.

If one controls the breath or Prana, the mind also is controlled. He who has controlled his mind has also controlled his breath. If one is suspended, the other is also suspended. If the mind and Prana are both controlled one gets liberation from the round of births and deaths and attains Immortality. There is intimate connection between the mind Prana and semen. If one controls the the seminal energy, the mind and Prana are also controlled. He who has controlled his seminal energy has also controlled his Prana and mind.

He who practises Pranayama will have good appetite, cheerfulness, handsome figure, good strength, courage, enthusiasm, a high standard of health, vigour and vitality and good concentration of mind. Pranayama is quite suitable for the Westerners also.

A Yogi measures the span of his life not by the number of years but by the numbers of his breaths. You can take in certain amount of energy or Prana from the atmospheric air along with each breath. Vital capacity is the capacity shown by the largest quantity of air a man can inhale after the deepest possible exhalation. A man takes fifteen breaths in a minute. The total number of breaths comes to 21,600 times per day.

Varieties of Pranyam

"*Bahya bhyantar-Stambha-vrittih desa kala-Sankhyabhih paridrishto dirghat Sukshamat.*"

Yoga Sutras—Chap. II Su. 50.

Pranayam is regarded lengthy or subtle according to its three components, the external, the internal and the steady or the retention processes are modified by the regulations of space, time and number.

When the breath is expired, it is Rechak, the first kind of Pranayam. When the breath is drawn in, it is the second, termed Purak. When it is suspended, it is the third kind, called Kumbhak. Kumbhak is retention of breath. Kumbhak increases the period of life. It augments the inner spiritual force, vigour and vitality. If you retain the breath for one minute, this one minute is added to your span of life. Yogins by taking the breath to the Brahmarandhra at the top of the head and keeping it there, defeat the Lord of death, Yama, and conquer death. Each of these motions in Pranayam *viz.*, Rechak, Purak, and Kumbhak, is regulated by space, time and number. By space is meant the inside or outside of the body and the particular length or the breadth and also when the Prana is held in some particular part of the body. During expiration the distance to which breath is thrown outside varies in different individuals. The distance varies during inspiration also. The length of the breath varies in accordance with the prevailing Tattwa. The length of the breath is respectively 12, 16, 4, 8, 0 finger breadths according the Tattwa Prithvi, Apas, Tejas, Vayu or Akasa (earth, water, fire, air or ether). This is again externally during exhalation and internally during inhalation.

Time is, the time of duration of each of these, which is generally counted by Matra, which corresponds to one second. Matra means a measure. By time is also meant how long the Prana should be fixed in a particular centre or part.

Number refers to the number of times the Pranayam is performed. The Yogic students should slowly take the number of Pranayam to eighty at one sitting. He should have four sittings in morning, afternoon, evening and mid-night, or at 9 p.m., and should have thus 320 Pranayams in all. The effect or fruit of Pranayam if Udgata or awakening of the sleeping Kundalini. The chief aim of Pranayam is to unite the Prana with the Apana and take the united Pranapana slowly upwards towards the head.

Kundalini is the source for all occult powers. The Pranayam is long or short according to the period of time, it is practised for. Just as water, thrown on a hot pan shrivels upon all sides, as it is being dried up, so also the air, moving in or out ceases its action by a strong effort of restraint (Kumbhak) and stay within.

Vachaspati describes—"Measured by 36 Matras, is the first attempt (Udagata), which is mild. Twice that is the second, which is middling. Thrice that is the third, which is the intense. This is the Pranayam as measured by number.

The 'place' of exhalation lies within 12 (Angulas) inches of the tip of nose. This is to be ascertained through a piece of reed or cotton. The place of inhalation ranges from the head down to the soles of the feet. This is to be ascertained through a sensation similar to the touch of an ant. The place of Kumbhak consists of the external and internal places of both exhalation and inhalation taken together, because the functions of the breath are capable of being held up at both these places. This is to be ascertained through the absence of the two indicatives noted above, in connection with exhalation and inhalation.

The specification of the 3 kinds of breath-regulations, by all these three—time, space and number—is only optional, They are not to be understood as to be practised collectively, for, in many Smiritis we meet with passages, where the only specification mentioned with reference to the regulation of breath is that of time.

The fourth is restraining the Prana by directing to external or internal object:—

"*Bahyabhyantar—visyakshepi—chaturthah*"

Yoga Sutras—Ch. II.

The third kind of Pranayam that is described in Sutra 50 of the Yoga Sutras, is practised only till the first Udagata is marked. This fourth Pranayam is carried further. It concerns with the fixing of the Prana in the various lotuses (Padmas or Chakras) and taking it slowly and slowly, step by step, and stage by stage to the last lotus in the head, where perfect Samadhi takes place. This is internal. Externally it takes into consideration the length of breath in accordance with the prevailing Tattwa. Prana can be directed either inside or outside.

By gradual mastery over the preliminary three kinds of Pranayam, the fourth kind comes in. In the third kind of Pranayam the sphere is not taken into consideration. The stoppage of the breath occurs with one single effort and is then measured by space, time and number and thus becomes Deergha (long) and Sukshama (subtle). In the fourth variety, however, the spheres of expiration and inspiration are ascertained. The different states are mastered by and by. This fourth variety is not practised all at once by a single effort like the third one. On the other hand, it reaches different states of perfection, as it is being done. After one stage is mastered, the next stage is taken up and practised. That it goes in succession. The third is not preceded by measurements and is brought about by a single effort. The fourth is however preceded by the knowledge of the measurements, and is brought about by much effort. This is the only difference. The conditions of time, space and number are applicable to this kind of Pranayam also. Particular occult powers develop themselves at each stage of progress.

Three Types of Pranayam

There are three types of Pranayam, *viz.*, Adhama, Madhyama and Uttama (inferior, middle and superior). The Adhama Pranayam consists of 12 Matras, Madhyama consists of 24 Matras and the Uttama occupies a time of 32 Matras. This is for Purak. The ratio between

Purak, Kumbhak and Rechak is 1: 4: 2. Purak is inhalation. Kumbhak is retention. Rechak is exhalation. If you inhale for a period of 12 Matras, you will have to make Kumbhak for a period of 48 Matras. Then the time for Rechak will be tor 24 Matras. This is for Adhama Pranayam. The same rule will apply to the other two varieties. First, practise for a month the Adhama Pranayam. Then practise Madhyama for three months. Then take up the Uttama variety.

Salute to your Guru and Sri Ganesh as soon as you sit on the Asan. The time for Abhyasa is early morning 4 a. m., 10 a.m., evening 5 p.m., and night 10 p.m., or 12 p.m. As you advance in practice you will have to do 320 Pranayam daily.

Sagarbha Pranayam is that Pranayam, which is attended with mental Japa of any Mantra, either Gayatri or OM. It is one hundred times more powerful than the Agarbha Pranayam, which is plain and unattended with any Japa.

Pranayam Siddhi depends upon the intensity of the efforts of the practitioner. An ardent enthusiastic student, with Parama Utsaho, Sahasa and Dridhata (zeal, cheerfullness and tenacity), can effect Siddhi (perfection) within six months; while a happy-go-lucky practitioner with Tandra and Alasya (drowsiness and laziness) will find no improvement even after 8 or 10 years. Plod on. Persevere with patience, faith, confidence, expectation, interest and attention. You are bound to succeed. *Nil desperandum*—Never despair.

The Vedantic Kumbhak

Being without any distraction and with a calm mind, one should practise Pranayam. Both expiration and inspiration should be stopped. The practitioner should depend solely on Brahman that is the highest aim of life. The giving out of all external object is said to be Rechak. The taking in of the spiritual knowledge of the Shastras is said to be Purak and the keeping to oneself of such knowledge is said to be Kumbhak.

He is an emancipated person who practises his Chitta thus. There is no doubt about it. Through Kumbhak, the mind should always be taken up and through Kumbhak alone it should be filled up within. It is only through Kumbhak that Kumbhak should be firmly mastered. Within it, is "Param-Siva." At first in his Brahmagranti there is produced soon a hole or passage. Then having pierced Brahmagranti, he pierces Vishnugranti, then he pierces Rudragranti, when to the Yogin comes Vedha (piercing) through his liberation from the impurities of delusion, through the religious ceremonies, performed in various births, through the grace of Gurus and Devatas and through the practice of Yoga.

Pranayam for Nadi Shuddhi

The Vayu cannot enter the Nadis if they are full of impurities. Therefore, first of all, they should be purified and then Pranayam should be practised. The Nadis are purified by two processes *viz.*, Samanu and Nirmanu. The Samanu is done by a mental process with Bija

Mantra. The Nirmanu is done by physical cleansing or the Shatkarmas.

1. Sit on Padmasan. Meditate on the Bijakshara of Vayu वं (*Vam*) which is of smoke colour. Inhale through the left nostril. Repeat the Bijakshara 16 times. This is Purak. Retain the breath till you repeat the Bija 64 times. This is Kumbhak. Then exhale through the right nostril very very slowly till you repeat the Bijakshara 32 times.

2. The navel is the seat of Agnitattwa. Meditate on this Agnitattwa. Then draw the breath through the right nostril repeating 16 times the Agni Bija रं (*Ram*). Retain the breath, till you count *Ram* 64 times. Then exhale slowly through the left nostril till you repeat mentally the Bija letter 32 times.

3. Fix the gaze at the tip of the moon there. Inhale through the left nostril repeating the Bija थं (*Tham*) 16 times. Retain the breath till you repeat the Bija Tham 64 times. Now imagine that the nectar that flows from the moon,

runs through all the vessels of the body and purifies them. Then exhale slowly through the right nostril till you repeat the Prithvi Bija लं (*Lam*) 32 times.

The Nadis are purified nicely by the practice of the above three kinds of Pranayam. Then practise the regular Pranayam by sitting firmly in your usual posture.

Pranayam Mantra

(Mantra during Pranayam)

"The Mantra for repetition during the practice of Pranayam is laid down in the Ishwar Gita. "When the aspirant holding his breath repeats the Gayatri thrice, together with the seven Vyakrities in the beginning; the Siras at the end and the Pranava, one at both ends of it, this is, what is called the regulation of breath."

Yogi Yajnavalkya, on the other hand, declares thus :—

"The upward breath and the downward breath, having been restrained, regulation of breath is to be practised by means of the Pranava "ॐ" with one regard to the unit of measure of the Matra."

This repetition of the Pranava "ॐ" alone, is meant for the Paramahamsa Sannyasis. It has been declared in the Smiritis, that ordinarily contemplation is to be practised, through the inhalation and other stages of breath regulation at one's navel, heart and forehead, with reference to the forms of Brahma, Vishnu and Siva respectively. For the Paramahamsas, however, the only object of contemplation has been declared to be Brahman. "The self-controlled ascetic is to contemplate upon the supreme Brahman, by means of the Pranava, declares the Sruti."

Exercise No. I.

Sit on Padmasan. Close your eyes. Concentrate on Trikuti (the space between the two eye-brows). Close the right nostril with your right thumb. Inhale slowly through the left nostril as long as you can do it with comfort. Then exhale very very slowly through the same nostril. Do twelve times. This is one round.

Then inhale through the right nostril by closing the left nostril with your right ring and little fingers and exhale very slowly through the same nostril. Do twelve times. This is one round.

Do not make any sound during inhalation and exhalation. Repeat your Ishta Mantra during the practice. In the second week of practice do two rounds, in the third week, three rounds. Take rest for two minutes when one round is over. If you take a few normal breaths when one round is over, that will give you sufficient rest and you will be fresh for the next round. There is no Kumbhak in this exercise. You can increase the number of rounds according to your strength and capacity.

Exercise No. 2.

Inhale through both the nostrils slowly and gently. Do not retain the breath. Then exhale slowly. Do 12 times. This will constitute one round. You can do 2 or 3 rounds according to your capacity and strength and time at your disposal.

Exercise No. 3.

Sit on your Asan. Close the right nostril with your right thumb. Then inhale slowly through your left nostril. Close the left nostril with your right ring and little fingers and open the right nostril by removing the right thumb. Exhale very slowly through the right nostril.

Then draw the air through the right nostril as long as you can do it with comfort and exhale through the left nostril by removing the right ring and little fingers. There is no Kumbhak in this Pranayama. Repeat the process 12 times. This will constitute one round.

Exercise No. 4.

Meditate that the single letter, the supreme light—the Pranava OM is the origin or source of these three letters

A, U, and M. Inhale the air through Ida or left nostril for the space of sixteen Matras (16 seconds), meditate on the letter 'A' during that time; retain the air for the space of 64 Matras (seconds), meditate on the letter 'U' during the time; exhale through the right nostril for the space of 32 Matras (seconds) and meditate on the letter 'M' during that time. Practise this again and again in the above order. Begin with 2 or 3 times and gradually increase the number to 20 or 30 times according to your capacity and strength. To begin with keep the ratio 1: 4: 2. Gradually increase the ratio to 16: 64: 32.

Deep Breathing Exercise

Each deep breathing consists of a very full inhalation, through the nose and a deep, steady exhalation also, through the nose.

Inhale slowly as much as you can do. Exhale slowly as much as you can do. During inhalation observe the following rules:—

1. *Stand up. Place the hands on the hips, the elbows will be out and not forced backwards. Stand at ease.*

2. Lengthen the chest straight upwards. Press the hip bones with the hands in a downward direction. A vacuum will be formed by this act and the air will rush in of its own accord.

3. Keep the nostrils wide open. Do not use the nose as a suction pump. It should serve as a passive passage for both the inhaled and the exhaled air, Do not make any sound when you inhale and exhale. Remember that correct breathing is noiseless.

4. Stretch the whole upper part of the trunk.

5. Do not arch the upper chest into a cramped position. Keep the abdomen naturally relaxed.

6. Do not bend the head far backwards. Do not draw the abdomen inwards. Do not force the shoulders back. Lift the shoulders up.

During exhalation observe the following rules carefully :—

1. Allow the ribs and the whole upper part of the trunk to sink down gradually.

2. Draw the lower ribs and abdomen upwards slowly.

3. Do not bend the body too much forward. Arching of the chest should be avoided. Keep the head, neck and trunk in a straight line. Contract the chest. Do not breathe the air out through the mouth. Exhale very, very slowly without producing any noise.

4. Expiration simply takes place by relaxing the inspiratory muscles. The chest falls down by its own weight and expels the air out through the nose.

5. In the beginning, do not retain the breath after inhalation. When the process of inhalation is over, begin exhalation at once. When you have sufficiently advanced in your practice, you can slowly retain the breath from 5

seconds to 1 minute according to your strength and capacity.

6. When one round of three deep breathings is over, you can take a little rest, "Respiratory pause"—by taking a few normal breaths. Then start the second round. During the pause, stand still in a comfortable position with hands on hips. The number of rounds can be fixed according to the capacity of the practitioner. Do 3 or 4 rounds and increase one round every week. Deep breathing is only a variety of Pranayam.

Kapalabhati

'*Kapala*' is a Sanskrit word. It means skull and '*Bhati*' means to shine. The term '*Kapalabhati*' means an exercise that makes the skull shine. This Kriya cleanses the skull. So, this is taken as one of the Shat Karmas (six cleansing processes in Hatha Yoga.

Sit on Padmasan. Keep the hands on knees. Close the eyes. Perform Purak and Rechak rapidly. This should be practised vigorously. One will get perspiration profusely. This is a good form of exercise. Those who are well-versed in Kapalabhati, can do Bhastrika very easily. There is no Kumbhak in this Pranayam. Rechak plays a prominent part. Purak is mild, slow and long (Dheerga). But the Rechak should be done quickly and forcibly by contracting the abdominal muscles with a backward push. When you do Purak, release the abdominal muscles. Some people naturally make a curve of the spine and bend their heads also. This is not desirable. The head and the trunk should be erect. Sudden expulsions of breath follow one another as in Bhastrika. To start with you can have one expulsion per second. Gradually you can have two expulsions per second. To begin with, do one round in the morning consisting of 10 expulsions only. In the second week, do one round in the evening. In the third week, do two rounds in the morning and two rounds in the evening. Thus every week gradully and cautiously increase 10 expulsions to each round till you get 120 expulsions for each round.

It cleanses the respiratory system and the nasal passages. It removes the spasm in bronchial tubes. Consequently Asthma is relieved and also cured in course of time. The apices of the lungs get proper oxygenation. Thereby they cannot afford favourable nidus (breeding grounds) for tubercle bacilli. Consumption is cured by this practice. Lungs are considerably developed. Carbon-di-oxide is eliminated in a large scale. Impurities of the blood are thrown out. Tissues and cells absorb a lare quantity of oxygen. The practitioner keeps up good health. Heart functions properly. The circulatory and respiratoy systems are toned to a considerable degree.

The External Kumbhak

(BAHYA)

Draw the air through the left nostril till you count 3 OMs; throw it out through the right nostril immediately without retaining it counting 6 OMs. Stop it outside till you count 12 OMs. Then draw the breath through the right; exhale it through the left and stop it outside as before, using the same units of OM for inhalation, exhalation and retention. Do six times in the morning and six times in the evening. Gradually increase the number of rounds and the time of Kumbhak. Do not strain or fatigue youself.

Easy Comfortable Pranayam
(SUKH PURVAK)

Sit on Padmasan or Siddhasan in your meditation room, before the picture of your Ishta Devata (guiding deity). Close the right nostril with the right thumb. Draw in the air very, very slowly through the left nostril. Then close the left nostril also with the little and ring fingers of the right hand. Retain the air as long as you can comfortably do. Then exhale very, very slowly through the right nostril after removing the thumb. Now half the process is over. Then draw the air through the right nostril. Retain the air as before and exhale it very, very slowly through the left nostril. All these six processes constitute one Pranayam. Do 20 in the morning and 20 in the evening. Gradually increase the number. Bave a Hhav (mental attitude) that all the Deivi Sampat (divine qualities) *e.g.*, mercy, love, forgiveness, Santi, joy, etc., are entering into your system along with the inspired air and all Asura Sampat (devilish qualities) such as lust, anger, greed, etc., are being thrown out along with the expired air. Repeat OM or Gayatri* Mentally during Purak, Kumbhak and Rechak, Hard-working Sadhaks can do 320 Kumbhaks daily in four sittings at the rate of 80 in each sitting.

This Pranayam removes all diseases, purifies the Nadis, steadies the mind in concentration, improves digestion, increases the digestive fire and the appetite, helps to maintain Brahmacharya and awakens the Kundalini that is sleeping at the Muladhara Chakra. Purification of Nadis will set in rapidly. You will have levitation (raising from the ground) also.

---

*Various Mantra and their benefits are described in "Yoga by Japa."

Pranayam for Awakening Kundalini

When you practise the following, concentrate on the Muladhara Chakra at the base of the spinal column, which is triangular in form and which is the seat of the Kundalini Shakti. Close the right nostril with your right thumb. Inhale through the left nostril till you count 3 OMs slowly. Imagine that you are drawing the Prana with the atmospheric air. Then close the left nostril with your little and ring fingers of the right hand. Then retain the breath for 12 OMs. Send the current down the spinal column straight into the triangular lotus, the Muladhara Chakra. Imagine that the nerve-current is striking against the lotus and awakening the Kundalini. Then slowly exhale through the right nostril counting 6 OMs. Repeat the process from the right nostril, as stated above, using the same units, and having the same imagination and feelings. This Pranayam will awaken the Kundalini quickly. Do it 3 times in the morning and 3 times in the evening. Increase the number and time gradually and cautiously according to your strength and capacity. In this Pranayam, concentration on the Muladhara Chakra is the importont thing. Kundalini will be awakened quickly if the degree of concentration is intense and if the Pranayam is practised regularly.

Pranayam during meditation

If you do concentration and meditation, Pranayam comes by itself. The breath becomes slower and slower. We all practise this Pranayam daily unconsciously. When you are reading a sensational story-book or when you are solving a mathematical problem, your mind is really very much absorbed in the subject matter. If you closely watch your breath on these occasions, you will find that the breath has become very, very slow. When you see a tragical story being enacted in the theatre or a film-show, when you hear a very sad striking news or some glad tidings, when you shed tears, either of joy or sorrow or burst into laughter, the breath is slackened. Pranayam comes by itself. In those Yogic students who practise Sirshasan, Pranayam comes by itself. It is obvious from these examples that when the mind is deeply concentrated on any subject, the respiration slows down or stops. Pranayam is done automatically. Mind and Prana are intimately connected. Prana is the over-coat for the mind. If you turn your attention to watch the breath on those occasions, it will regain its normal state. Pranayam comes by itself to those who are deeply absorbed in doing Japa, Dhyana or Brahma Vichara (enquiry of Atma.)

Prana, mind and Veerya (seminal energy) are under one Sambandha (connection). If you can control the mind, Prana and Veerya are controlled by themselves. If you can control Prana, mind and Veerya are controlled by themselves. If you control the Veerya by remaining as an Akhanda Brahmachari without emission of even a single drop of semen for 12 years, mind and Prana are controlled by themselves. Just as there is connection between wind and fire (light), so also there is connection between Prana and mind. Wind fans the fire. Prana also fans the mind. If there is no wind, fire or light gets steady. Hatha Yogis approach Brahman by controlling Prana. Raja Yogis approach Brahman by controlling mind.

In this Pranayam you need not close the nostrils. Simply close the eyes if you practise it in a sitting posture. Forget the body and concentrate. If you practise this during walking, just feel minutely the cool air that is inhaled and exhaled.

Pranayam while Walking

Walk with head up, shoulders back and with chest expanded. Inhale slowly through both nostrils counting OM mentally 3 times, one count for each step. Then retain the breath till you count 12 OMs. Then exhale slowly through both nostrils till you count 6 OMs. Take the respiratory pause or rest after one Pranayam counting 12 OMs. If you find it difficult to count OM with each step, count OM without having any concern with the steps.

Kapalabhati can also be done during walking. Those who are very busy can practise the above Pranayam during their morning and evening walks. It is like killing two birds with one stone. You will find it very pleasant to practise Pranayam while walking in an open place, when delightful gentle breeze is blowing. You will be invigorated and innervated quickly to a considerable degree. Practise, feel and realise the marked, beneficial influence of this kind of Pranayam. Those who walk briskly, repeating OM mentally or verbally, do practise natural Pranayam without any effort. Sri Ganga Shankarji of Rishikesh does this daily.

Pranayam in Savasan

Lie down on the back, quiet at ease, over a blanket. Keep the hands on the ground by the sides and the legs straight. The heels should be kept together, but the toes can remain a little apart. Relax all the muscles and the nerves. Those who are very weak, can practise Pranayam in this pose while lying on the ground or on a bedstead. Draw the breath slowly without making any noise, through both nostrils. Retain the breath as long as you can do it with comfort. Then exhale slowly through both nostrils. Repeat the process 12 times in the morning and 12 times in the evening. Chant OM mentally during the practice. If you like you can practise the: "Easy Comfortable Pranayam" in this posture also (vide page 133). This is a combined exercise on Asan, Pranayam, meditation and rest. It gives rest not only to the body but also for the mind. It gives relief, comfort and ease. This is very much suited for aged people.

Rhythmical Breathing

The breathing in men and women is very irregular. In exhalation the Prana goes out 16 digits and in inhalation only 12 digits, thus losing 4 digits. But if you inhale for 16 digits as in exhalation, then you will have rhythmical breathing. The the power. Kundalini, will be roused. By practice of rhythmical breathing you will enjoy real good rest. You can control the respiratory centre that is situated in medulla oblongata and other nerves also, because the centre of respiration has a sort of controlling effect on other nerves. He who has calm nerves, has a calm mind also.

If the units of exhalation and inhalation are the same, you will have rhythmical breathing. If you inhale till you count 6 OMs, exhale also till you count 6 OMs. This is breathing in and out in a measured manner. This will harmonise the whole system. This will harmonise the physical body, mind, Indriyas and will soothe the tired nerves. You will experience full repose and calmness. All the bubbling emotions will subside and the surging impulses will calm down.

There is another variety of modification of rhythmic breathing. Inhale slowly through both nostrils for 4 OMs; retain the breath for 8 OMs (internal Kumbhak); exhale slowly through both nostrils for 4 OMs; and retain the breath outside (external Kumbhak) for 8 OMs.

Repeat the above process a number of times according to your strength and capacity. You can gradually increase the duration of inhalation and exhalation after some practice to 8 OMs and the period between breaths to 16 OMs. But never try to increase the duration until you are sure that you have power and strength to do so. You must experience joy and pleasure in doing the same. You should not feel any undue strain. Pay considerable attention to keep up the rhythm. Remember that the rhythm is more important than the length of breath. You must feel the rhythm throughout your whole body. Practice will make you perfect. Patience and perseverance are needed.

Surya Beda

Sit on Padmasan or Siddhasan. Close the eyes. Keep the left nostril closed with your right ring and the little fingers. Slowly inhale without making any sound as long as you can do it comfortably through the right nostril. Then close the right nostril with your right thumb and retain the breath by firmly pressing the chin against the chest, Jalandhara Bandha. Hold on the breath till perspiration oozes from the tips of the nails and the roots of the hairs (hair follicles). This point cannot be reached at the very outset. You will have to increase the period of Kumbhak gradually. This is the limit of the sphere of practice of Surya Beda Kumbhak. Then exhale very slowly without making any sound through the left nostril by closing the right nostril with the thumb. Repeat OM mentally with Bhav and meaning during inhalation, retention and exhalation. Exhale after purifying the skull by forcing the breath up.

This Pranayam should again and again be performed, as it purifies the brain and destroys the intestinal worms and diseases arising from excess of wind, Vayu. This removes the four kinds of evils caused by Vayu and cures Vata, Rheumatism. It cures rhinitis of the cephalalgia and various sorts of neuralgia. The worms that are found in the frontal sinuses are removed. It destroys decay and death, awakens the Kundalini Shakti and increases the bodily fire.

Ujjayi

Sit in Padmasan or Siddhasan. Close the mouth. Inhale slowly through both the nostrils in a smooth, uniform manner till the breath fills the space from the throat to the heart.

Retain the breath as long as you can do it comfortably and then exhale slowly through the left nostril by closing the right nostril with your right thumb. Expand the chest when you inhale. During inhalation a peculiar sound is produced owing to the partial closing of glottis. The sound produced during inhalation should be of a mild and uniform pitch. It should be continuous also. This Kumbhak may be practised even when walking or standing. Instead of exhaling through the left nostril, you can exhale slowly through both nostrils,

This removes the heat in the head. The practitioner becomes very beautiful.

The gastric fire is increased. It removes all the evils arising in the body and the Dhatus and Jalodhara (dropsy of the belly or ascites). It removes phlegm in the throat, asthma, consumption and all sorts of pulmonary diseases are cured. All diseases that arise from deficient inhalation of oxygen, diseases of the heart are cured. All works are accomplished by Ujjayi Pranayam. The practitioner is never attacked by diseases of phlegm, nerves, dyspepsia, dysentery, enlarged spleen, consumption, cough or fever. Perform Ujjayi to destroy decay and death.

Sitkari

Fold the tongue so that the tip of the tongue might touch the upper palate and draw the air through the mouth with a hissing sound C C C C C (or *Si. Si, Si, Si*). Then retain the breath as long as you can without the feeling of suffocation and then exhale slowly through both nostrils. You can keep the two rows of teeth in contact and then inhale the air through the mouth as before.

This practice enhances the beauty of the practitioner and vigour of his body. It removes hunger, thirst, indolence and sleep. His strength will be just like that of Indra. He becomes the lord of Yogis. He is able to do and undo things. He becomes an independent monarch. He becomes invincible. No injury will affect him. When you are thirsty practise this. You will be relieved of thirst immediately.

Sitali

Protrude the tongue a little away from the lips. Fold the tongue like a tube. Draw in the air through the mouth with the hissing sound *Si*. Retain the breath as long as you can hold on with comfort. Then exhale slowly through both nostrils. Practise this daily again and again in the morning from 15 to 30 times. You can do this either on Padmasan, Siddhasan, Vajrasan or even when you stand or walk.

This Pranayam purifies the blood. It quenches thirst and appeases hunger. It cools the system. It destroys gulma (chronic dyspepsia), pleeha, inflammation of various chronic diseases, fever, consumption, indigestion, bilious disorders, phlegm, the bad effects of poison, snake bite, etc. When you are caught up in a jungle or any place where you cannot get water, if you feel thirsty, practise this Pranayam. You will be at once relieved of thirst. He who practises this Pranayam regularly, will not be affected by the bite of serpents and scorpions. Sitali Kumbhak is an imitation of the respiration of a serpent. The practitioner gets the power of casting his skin and enduring the privation of air, water and food. He becomes a proof against all sorts of inflammations and fever.

Bastrika

In Sanskrit Bhastrika means 'bellows.' Rapid succession of forcible expulsions is a characteristic feature of Bhastrika. Just as a blacksmith blows his bellows rapidly so also you should move your breath rapidly.

Sit on Padmasan. Keep the body, neck and head erect. Close the mouth. Next inhale and exhale quickly twenty times like the bellows of the blacksmith. Constantly dilate and contract. When you practise this Pranayam a hissing sound is produced. The practitioner should start with rapid expulsions of breath following one another in rapid succession. When the required number of expulsions, say twenty for a round, is finished the final expulsion is followed by a deepest possible inhalation. The breath is suspended as long as it could be done with comfort. Then deepest possible exhalation is done very slowly. The end of this deep exhalation completes one round of Bhastrika. Rest a while after one round is over by taking a few normal breaths. This will give you relief and make you fit for starting the second round. Do three rounds daily in the morning. You can do another three rounds in the evening also. Busy people who find it difficult to do three rounds of Bhastrika daily, can do one round at least. This also will keep them quite fit.

Bhastrika is a powerful exercise. A combination of Kapalabhati and Ujjayi makes up Bhastrika. Then you will find it very easy to do Bhastrika. Practise Kapalabhati and Ujjayi to start with.

Some prolong the practice till they get tired. You will get perspiration profusely. If you experience any giddiness stop the practice and take a few normal breaths. Continue the practice after the giddiness has vanished. Bhastrika can be done both in the morning and evening in winter. In summer do it in the morning only during cool hours.

Bhastrika relieves inflammation of the throat, increases gastric fire, destroys phlegm, removes diseases of the nose and chest and eradicates asthma, consumption, etc. It gives good appetite. It breaks the three Granthis or knots, *viz.*, Brahma Granthi, Vishnu Granthi and Rudra Granthi. It destroys phlegm which is the bolt or obstacle to the door at the mouth of Brahma Nadi (Sushumna). It enables one to know the Kundalini. It removes all diseases which arise from excess of wind, bile and phlegm. It gives warmth to the body. When you have no sufficient warm clothing in a cold region to protect yourself from cold, practise this Pranayam and you will get sufficient warmth in the body quickly. It purifies the Nadis considerably. It is the most beneficial of all Kumbhaks. Bhastrika Kumbhak should be specially practised as it enables the Prana to break through the three Granthis or knots that are firmly located in the Sushumna. It awakens the Kundalini quickly. The practitioner will never suffer from any disease. He will always be healthy.

The number of exhalations or rounds is determined by the strength and capacity of the practitioner. You must not go to extremes. Some students do six rounds. Some do twelve also.

You can practise Bhastrika in the following manner. There is some slight change in the end. Having inhaled and exhaled quickly twenty times, inhale through the right nostril, retain the breath as long as you can do it comfortably and then exhale through the left nostril. Then inhale through the left nostril, retain the breath as before and then exhale through the right nostril.

Repeat OM mentally with Bhav and meaning throughout the practice.

There are some varieties of Bhastrika wherein one nostril only is used for breathing purposes and in another variety the alternate nostrils are used for inhalation and exhalation.

Bhramari

Sit on Padmasan or Siddhasan. Inhale rapidly through both nostrils making the sound of *Chrawar*, the bee, and exhale rapidly through both nostrils, making the humming sound.

You can carry the process till the body is bathed in perspiration. In the end inhale through both nostrils retain the breath as long as you can do it comfortably and then exhale slowly through both nostrils. The joy which the practitioner gets in making this Kumbhak is unlimited and indescribable. In the beginning, heat of the body is increased as the circulation of blood is quickened. In the end the bodily heat is decreased by perspiration. By success in this Bhramari Kumbhak, the Yogic student gets success in Samadhi.

Murcha

Sit in your Asan and inhale. Retain the breath. Do Jalandhara Bandha by pressing the chin against the chest. Retain the breath till you expect fainting and then exhale slowly. This is Murcha Kumbhak as it makes the mind senseless and gives happiness. But this is not suitable for many.

Plavini

Practise of this Pranayam demands skill on the part of the student. He who practises this Plavini can do Jalasthamba and float on water for any length of time. Mr. 'S' a Yogic student can float on water for twelve hours at a stretch. He who practises this plavini Kumbhak can live on air and dispense with food for some days. The student actually drinks air like water slowly and sends it to the stomach. The stomach gets bloated a bit. If you tap the stomach when it is filled with air, you will get a peculiar tympanic (air) sound. Gradual practice is necessary. The help of one who is well versed in this Pranayam is also necessary. The student can expel all the air from the stomach by gradual belching.

Kevala Kumbhak

Kumbhak is of two kinds, *viz.*, Sahita and Kevala. That which is coupled with inhalation and exhalation is termed Sahita. That which is devoid of these is called Kevala (alone). When you get mastery in Sahita, then you can attempt for this Kevala. When in due course of practice, "Sahita Kumbhak" lasts for months and years together and subsists in many places without exhalation and inhalation and without conditioned by place, time and number—then that Kumbhak is called absolute and pure (Kevala Kumbhak), the fourth form of 'Regulation of breath'. Such powers as that of roaming about in space unseen follow this last form of Pranayam. In Vasishta Samhita it is said: "When after giving up inhalation and exhalation, one holds his breath with ease, it is absolute Kumbhak (Kevala.") In this Pranayam the breath is suddenly stopped without Purak and Rechak. The student can restrain his breath as long as he likes through this Kumbhak. He attains the state of Raja Yoga. Through Kevala Kumbhak, the knowledge of Kundalini arises. Kundalini is aroused and the Sushumna is free from all sorts of obstacles. He attains perfection in Hatha Yoga. You can practise this Kumbhak three times a day. He who knows Pranayam and Kevala is the real Yogi. What can he not accomplish in the three worlds, who has acquired success in this Kevala Kumbhak? Glory, glory to such exalted souls. This Kumbhak cures all diseases and promotes longevity.

Pranic Healing

Those who practise Pranayam, can impart their Prana in healing morbid diseases. They can also recharge themselves with Prana in no time by practising Kumbhak. Never think that you will be depleted of your Prana by distributing it to others. The more you will give, the more it will flow to you from the cosmic source (*Hiranyagarbha*). That is the law of nature. Do not become a niggard. If there is a rheumatic patient, gently shampoo his legs with your hands. When you do shampooing (massage), do Kumbhak and imagine that the Prana is flowing from your hands towards the leg of your patients. Connect yourself with Hiranyagarbha or the cosmic Prana and imagine that the cosmic energy is flowing through your hands towards the legs of the patient. The patient will at once feel warmth, relief and strength. You can cure headache, intestinal colic or any other disease by massage and by your magnetic touch. When you massage the liver, spleen, stomach or any other portion or organ of the body, you can speak to the cells and give them orders :— "Oh cells! Discharge your functions properly. I command you to do so." They will obey your orders. They too have got sub-conscious intelligence. Repeat OM when you pass your Prana to others. Try a few cases. You will gain competence. You can cure scorpion-sting also. Gently shampoo the leg and bring the poison down.

You can have extraordinary power of concentration, strong will and a perfectly, healthy, strong body by practising Pranayam regularly. You will have to direct the power or Prana consciously to unhealthy parts of the body. Suppose you have a sluggish liver. Sit on Padmasan. Close your eyes. Inhale gently till you count OM 3 times. Then retain the breath till you count OM 6 times. Direct the Prana to the region of the liver. Concentrate your mind there. Fix your attention to that area. Imagine that Prana is inter-penetrating all the tissues and the cells of the lobes of the liver and doing its curative, regenerating and constructive work there. Faith. imagination, attention and interest play a very important part in curing diseases by taking Prana to the diseased areas. Then slowly exhale. During exhalation imagine that the morbid impurities of the liver are thrown out. Repeat this process 12 times in the morning and 12 times in the evening. Sluggishness of liver will vanish in a few days. This is a drugless treatment. This is nature cure. You can take the Prana to any part of the body during Pranayam and cure any kind of disease, be it acute or chronic. Try once or twice in healing yourself. Your convictions will grow stronger. Why do you cry like the lady who is crying for ghee when she has butter in her hand, when you have a cheap, potent, easily available remedy or agent Prana at you command at all times! Use it judiciously. When you advance in your concentration and practice, you can cure many diseases by mere touch. In the advanced stages, many diseases are cured by mere will.

Distant Healing

This is known as "absent treatment" also. You can transit your Prana through space, to your friend, who is living at a distance. He should have a receptive mental attitude. You must feel yourself *en rapport* (in direct relation and in sympathy) with the man, whom you heal with this Distant Healing method.

You can fix hours of appointment with them through correspondence. You can write to them: "Get ready at 4 A.M. Have a receptive mental attitude. Lie down in an easy chair. Close your eyes. I shall transmit my Prana." Say mentally to the patient: "I am transmitting a supply of Prana (vital force)." Do Kumbhak when you send the Prana. Practise rhythmical breathing also. Have a mental image that the Prana is leaving your mind when you exhale; it is passing through space and is entering the system of the patient. The Prana travels unseen like the wireless (radio) waves and flashes like lightning across space. The Prana that is coloured by the thought of the healer is projected outside. You can recharge yourself with Prana by practising Kumbhak. This requires long, steady, regular practice.

Relaxation

The practice of relaxing the muscles of the body will bring rest to the body and to the mind also. The tension of the muscles will be relieved. People who know the science of relaxation do not waste any energy. They can meditate well. Take a few deep breaths and then lie down flat on your back as in Savasan. Relax all the muscles of the body from head to feet. Roll on to one side and then relax as thoroughly as you can. Do not strain the muscles. Roll on the other side and relax. This is naturally done by all during sleep. There are various exercises in relaxation, for the particular muscles of a particular part of the body. You can relax the head, the shoulders, the arms, fore-arms, wrist, fingers, thighs, legs, ankles, toes, knees, elbows, wrist, etc. Yogis know the science of Relaxation thoroughly. When you practise these various relaxation exercises, you must have the mental picture of calmness and strength.

Relaxation of Mind

Mental poise and calmness may be brought about by the eradication of worry and anger. Fear really underlies both worry and anger. Nothing is gained by worry and anger, but on the contrary much energy is wasted by these two kinds of lower emotions. If a man worries much and if he is irritable, he is indeed a very weak man. Be careful and thoughtful. All unnecessary worries can be avoided. Relaxation of the muscles reacts on the mind and brings repose to the mind. Relaxation of the mind brings rest to the body also. Body and mind are intimately connected. Body is a mould prepared by the mind for its enjoyment.

Sit for 15 minutes in a relaxed and easy comfortable position. Close your eyes. Withdraw the mind from outside objects. Still the mind. Silence the bubbling thoughts. Think that the body is like a cocoanut shell and you are entirely different from the body. Think that the body is an instrument in your hands. Identify yourself with the all-pervading Spirit or Atma. Imagine that the whole world and your body are floating like a piece of straw, in this vast ocean of spirit. Feel that you are in touch with the Supreme Being. Feel that the life of the whole world is pulsating, vibrating and throbbing through you. Feel that the ocean of life is gently rocking you on its vast bosom. Then open your eyes. You will experience immense mental peace, mental vigour and mental strength. Practise and feel this.

Importance and Benefits of Pranayam

"The illusory Samsaric Vasana that has arisen through the practice of many lives, never perishes except through the practice of YOGA for a long time....... It is not possible on the part of one to control the mind by sitting up again and again except through the approved means."

(Muktikopanishad)

"How could Jnana capable of giving Moksha arise certainly without Yoga? And even Yoga becomes powerless in securing Moksha when it is devoid of

Jnana. So the aspirant after emancipation should practise (firmly) both Yoga and Jnana."

(Yogatattwa Upa.)

"*Tadah kshiyate prakashavaranam*—Thence the covering of light is destroyed."

(Yoga Sutras II—52)

Tamas and Rajas constitute the covering or veil. This veil is removed by the practice of Pranayam. After the veil is removed, the real nature of the soul is realised. The *Chitta* is by itself made up of Sattwic particles, but it is enveloped by Rajas and Tamas, just as the fire is enveloped by smoke. There is no purificatory action greater than Pranayam. Pranayam gives Purity and the light of knowledge shines. The Karma of the Yogi, which covers up the discriminative knowledge is destroyed as he practises Pranayam. By the magic panorama of desire. the essence, which is luminous by nature is covered up and the Jiva or individual soul is directed towards vice. This Karma of the Yogi which cover up the Light and binds him to repeated births, becomes attenuated by practice of Pranayam every moment and is destroyed eventually. The afflictions and sins constitute the cover according to Vachaspati.

Manu says: "Let the defects be burnt up by Pranayam." Vishnu Purana speaks of Pranayam as an accessory of Yoga: "He who wants the air known as Prana by practice is said to have secured Pranayam."

"*Dharnasu Yogyata Manasah*—The mind becomes fit for concentration" (Yoga Sutras: II—53). You will be able to concentrate the mind, nicely after this veil of the light has been removed. The mind will be quite steady like the flame in a windless place as the disturbing energy has been removed. The word Pranayam is sometimes used collectively for inhalation, retention and exhalation of breath and sometimes for each of these severally. When the Prana Vayu moves in the Akasa Tattwa, the breathing will be lessened. At this time it will be easy to stop the breath. The velocity of the mind will be slowly lessened by Pranayam. It will induce Vairag also.

If you can suspend one inch or digit of breath inside, you will obtain the powers of foretelling; if you can suspend two inches within, you will get the power of thought-reading; for suspending the breath for three inches, levitation; for four inches, psychometry, clairaudience, etc., for five inches, moving about unseen by anybody in the world; for six inches, the power Kaya Siddhi; for seven inches, entering the body of another man (Para-kaya-Pravesha); for eight inches, the power to remain always young; for nine inches, the power to make Devas to work as your servants; for ten inches, Anima, Mahima and other Siddhis; and for eleven inches, you will attain oneness with Paramatma. When through great practice the Yogi can perform Kumbhak for full three hours, then he can balance himself on his thumb. He undoubtedly attains all kinds of Siddhis. Just as fire destroys the fuel, so also Pranayam destroys the bundles of sins. Pratyahara makes the mind calm. Dharana steadies the mind. Dhayana makes one to forget the body and the world. Samadhi brings Infinite Bliss, Knowledge, Peace and Liberation.

"*Shastum thalu Shakram tatra amrita tadhara pravaha,*
Kantika moolarandhra rajatanti sandhini vivardhwaram,
Tatra sunyam dhyayet chitlayo bhavati."

During Yogic Samadhi, the flame of the Yogagni (fire of Yoga) extending from navel to the head melts the Amrita in the Brahmarandhra. The Yogi drinks this with joy and ecstasy. He can remain without food and drink for months by drinking this Yogic nectar alone.

The body becomes lean, strong and healthy. Too much fat is reduced. There is lustre in the face. Eyes sparkle like a diamond. The practitioner becomes very handsome. Voice becomes sweet and melodious. The inner Anahata sounds are distinctly heard. The student is free from all sorts of diseases. He gets established in Brahmacharya. Semen gets firm, steady. The Jataragni (gastric fire) is augmented. The student becomes so perfected in Brahmacharya that his mind will not be shaken even if a fairy tries to embrace him. Appetite becomes keen. Nadis are purified. The Vikshep is removed and the mind becomes one-pointed. Rajas and Tamas are destroyed. The mind is prepared for Dharana and Dhyan. The excretions become scanty. Steady practice arouses the inner spiritual light, happiness and peace of mind. It makes him an Oordhva-reta Yogi. Advanced students only will get all the other Siddhis, mentioned above.

The mind of a man can be made to transcend ordinary experience and exist on a plane higher than that of reason known as super-conscious state of concentration and gets beyond the limit of concentration. He comes face to face with facts which ordinary consciousness cannot comprehend. This ought to be achieved by proper training and manipulation of the subtle forces of the body so as to cause them to give, as it were, an upward push to the mind into the higher regions. When the mind is so raised into the super-conscious state of perception, it begins to act from there and experiences higher facts and higher knowledge. Such is the ultimate object of Yoga, which can be achieved by the practice of Pranayam. The control of the vibratory Prana means to a Yogi, the kindling of the fire of supreme knowledge, the realisation of the Self.

SPECIAL INSTRUCTIONS

1. Early morning answer the calls of nature and sit for the practice. Practise Pranayam in a dry, well-ventilated room. Pranayam requires deep concentration and attention. It is always better to have the practice in a steady sitting posture. Do not keep any one by your side to avoid distraction of your mind.

2. Before you sit for Pranayam practice, thoroughly clean the nostrils well. You can take a small quantity of fruit juice or a small cup of milk or coffee even before the practice. When you finish the practice, take a cup of milk or light tiffin after 10 minutes.

3. Have one sitting only in the morning during summer. If there is heat in the brain or head, apply *Amalaka* oil or butter on the head before you take your bath. Take *Misre Sharbat* by dissolving sugarcandy in water. This will cool your whole system. Do Sitali Pranayam also. You will not be affected by the heat.

4. Strictly avoid too much talking, eating, sleeping, mixing with friends and exertion. "Verily Yoga is not for him who eateth too much, nor who abstaineth to excess, nor even to wakefulness" (Gita VI-16). Take a little ghee with rice when you take your meals. This will lubricate the bowels and allow Vayu to move downwards freely.

5. **Mithaharam vina yasthu Yogarambham tu karayet,**
Nanarago Bhavettasya Kinchit yoge na Sidhyati.

(Ghe. S. Chap. V—16)

Without observing moderation of diet, if one takes to the Yoga practices, he cannot obtain any benefit but gets various diseases.

6. Perfect celibacy for six months or one year will doubtless enable you to acquire rapid progress in the practice and in spiritual advancement. Do not talk with ladies. Do not laugh and joke with them. Shun their company entirely. Without Brahmacharya and dietetic regulations if you practise Yogic exercises, you will not get maximum benefit in

the spiritual practices. But, for ordinary health you can practise mild exercises.

7. Be regular and systematic in your practice. Never miss a day. Stop the practice when you are ailing seriously. Some people twist the muscles of the face when they do Kumbhak. It should be avoided. It is a symptom to indicate that they are going beyond their capacity. This must be strictly avoided. Such people cannot have a regulated Rechak and Purak.

8. Obstacles in Yoga: "Sleeping in day time. late vigil over night, excess of urine and faeces, evil of unwholesome food, and laborious mental operation with Prana." When one is attacked by any disease, he says that the disease is due to the practice of Yoga. This is a serious mistake.

9. Get up at 4 a.m. Meditate or do Japa for half an hour. Then do Asans and Mudras. Take rest for 15 minutes. Then do Pranayam. Physical exercises can be conveniently combined with Asans. If you have sufficient time at

your disposal, yon can have it after finishing all the Yogic exercises and meditation. Pranayam can also be performed as soon as you get up from bed just before Japa and meditation. It will make your body light and you will enioy the meditation. You must have a routine according to your convenience and time.

10. Maximum benefit can be derived if Japa also is done during the practice of Asans and Pranayams.

11. It is always better to start Japa and meditation in the early morning at 4 a.m. as soon as you get up from bed. At this time the mind is quite calm and refreshed. You can have a good concentration.

12. Vast majority of persons waste their precious time in the early morning in answering the calls of nature for half an hour and washing their teeth for another half an hour. This is bad. Aspirants should try to defaecate within five minutes and cleanse their teeth within five minutes. If the bowels are

constipated, have vigorous practice of Salab, Bhujang and Dhanur Asans for five minutes as soon as you get up from bed. If you are habituated to answer the calls of nature, you can do so after finishing the Yogic exercises.

13. First do Japa and meditation. Then you can take to Asan and Pranayam exercises. Then finish the course of practice by another short sitting in meditation.

14. As there is always some drowsiness when you get up from bed, it is desirable to do some Asan and a little Pranayam for five minutes just to drive off this drowsiness and to make you fit for meditation. The mind gets one-pointed after the practice of Pranayam. Pranayam though it concerns with the breath, gives good exercise for the various internal organs and the whole body.

15. The general order of doing Kriyas is: First do all Asans, then Mudras, then Pranayam and then Dhyana. Since the early morning time is suitable for meditation, you can follow

this order: Japa, Meditation, Asans, Mudras and Pranayam. This is a better way. You can follow the order that which is suitable to you. After doing Asans, take rest for five minutes and then begin Pranayam.

16. Some Hatha Yogic books interdict cold bath in the early morning. Probably the reason may be that one may catch cold or develop any complaint of the lungs, if he takes cold bath at 4 a.m. particularly in cold places like Kashmere, Mussorie, Darjeeling, etc. There is no restriction in hot places. I am always in favour of morning cold baths before one starts the Yogic practices as it is refreshing and stimulating. It drives off drowsiness. It brings in equilibrium of circulation of blood. There is a healthy flow of blood towards the brain.

17. Asans and Pranayams remove all sorts of diseases, improve health, energise digestion, invigorate the nerves, straighten the Sushumna Nadi, remove Rajas and awaken Kundalini. Practice of Asans and Pranayams bestows good

health and a steady mind. As no Sadhana is possible without good health and as no meditation is possible without a steady mind, Hatha Yoga is of immense use for Dhyana Yogis, Karma Yogis, Bhaktas and Vedantis as well.

18. The maintenance of body is impossible without Asans or any kind of physical exercise or activities. Even an orthodox Vedanti is an unconscious Hatha Yogi. He practises some kind of Asan daily. He practises Pranayam also unconsciously because during meditation, Pranayam comes by itself.

19. Whenever you feel uneasy, depressed or dejected, practise Pranayam. You will be at once filled with new vigour, energy and strength. You will be elevated, renovated and filled with joy. Do this and try, Before you begin to write something, an essay, an article or a theises, do Pranayam first. You will bring out beautiful ideas and it will be an inspiring, powerful and original production.

20. Be regular in the practice. Regularity in the practice is very necessary if one wants to realise the maximum benefits of Asan, Pranayam. Those who practise by fits and starts will not derive any benefit. Generally people practise for two months in the beginning with great enthusiasm and leave off the practice. This is a sad mistake. They always want a Yogic teacher by their side. They have got the effiminate leaning mentality. They are lazy, torpid and slothful.

21. People do not want to remove Mala (impurity) by self-less service and Vikshep by Yogic practices. They at once jump to awake the Kundalini and raise Brahmakara Vritti. They will only break down their legs. Those who attempt to awake the Kundalini by Asans and Pranayams, should have purity in thought, word and deed. They should have mental and physical Brahmacharya. Then only they can enjoy the benefits of awakening the Kundalini.

22. Sow the seed of spirituality in your young age. Do not waste Veerya,

Discipline the Indriyas and mind. Do Sadhan. When you become old, it will be difficult for you to do any rigid Sadhan. Therefore be on the alert during your teens. You will see for yourself in a short time the particular benefits you derive from particular kinds of Sadhan.

23. When you advance in spiritual practices, you must observe strict Mowna (vow of silence) for 24 hours continuously. This must be continued for some months also. Everyone should select a course of few exercises in Asan, Pranayam, and meditation according to his temperament, capacity, convenience and requirement.

24. It is quite possible for a man to practise celibacy, albeit there are various sorts of temptations and distractions. A well-disciplined life, study of scriptures, Sat Sang, Japa, Dhyana, Pranayam, Sattwic and moderate diet, daily introspection and enquiry. self-analysis and self-correction. Sadachara, practice of Yama, Niyama, physical and

verbal Tapas all will pave a long way in the attainment of this end. People have irregular, unrighteous, immoderate, irreligious, undisciplined life. Hence they suffer and fail in the attainment of the goal of life. Just as the elephant throws sand on its own head, so also they themselves bring difficulties and troubles on their own heads on account of their foolishness.

25. Do not shake the body unnecessarily. By shaking the body often the mind also is disturbed. Do not scratch the body every now and then. The Asan should be steady and firm as a rock when you do Pranayam, Japa and Meditation.

26. You must find out for yourself according to your health and constitution what sort of dietetic regulation will suit and what particular Pranayam will exactly help you. Then only you can safely proceed with your Sadhan. First read all the instructions of the various exercises given in this book from the beginning to the end. Clearly understand

the technique. If you have doubts, just ask any Yogic student to demonstrate and then practise it. This is the safest method. You should not select any one of the exercises at random and begin to practise it in a wrong way.

27. In all the exercises I have observed Mantra "OM" to have a time-unit. You can have your Guru Mantra. Rama, Siva, Gayatri or mere number of any other time unit according to your inclination. Gayatri or OM is the best for Pranayam. In the beginning you must observe some time-unit for Purak, Kumbhak and Rechak. The time-unit and the proper ratio comes by itself when you do the Purak, Kumbhak and Rechak as long as you can do it comfortably. When you have advanced in the practice, you need not count or keep any unit. You will be naturally established in the normal ratio through force of habit.

28. For some days in the beginning you must count the number and see how you progress. In the advanced stages, you need not distract the mind in

counting. The lungs will tell you when the required number is finished.

29. Do not perform the Pranayam till you are fatigued. There must be always joy and exhilaration of spirit during and after the practice. You should come out of the practice fully invigorated and refreshed. Do not bind yourself by too many rules (Niyams).

30. Do not take bath immediately after Pranayam is over. Take rest for half an hour. If you get perspiration during the practice, do not wipe it with a towel. Rub it with your hands. Do not expose the body to the chill, draughts of air when you perspire.

31. Always inhale and exhale very slowly. Do not make any sound. In Pranayams like Bhastrika, Kapalabhati, Sitali and Sitkari you can produce a little mild or the lowest possible sound.

32. You should not expect the benefits after doing it for 2 or 3 minutes only for a day or two. At least you must have 15 minutes daily practice in the beginning regularly for days together.

There will be no use if you jump from one exercise to another everyday. You must have a particular exercise for your daily Abhyas, which you should improve to a high degree. Other exercises, of course, you can have for occasional practice along with the daily exercise. You must have Bhastrika, Kapalabhati and 'Easy Comfortable Pranayam' for your daily practice; and Sitali, Sitkari, etc., can be practised occasionally.

33. The Purak is otherwise known as 'Niswasa' and Rechak is known as 'Uchwasa.' The mental process in Kevala Kumbhak is called 'Sunyaka form' of breath regulation. Steady, systematic practice and gradual increase of Kumbhak is known as "Abhyasa Yoga." Swallowing of air and living on this air alone is known as 'Vayubhakshan.'

34. The author of Sivayoga Dipika describes three kinds of Pranayam: Prakrita, Vaikrita and Kevala Kumbhak. "If the Prana is in the form of breath inhaled and exhaled. on account of its natural quality of going out and coming

in, the Pranayam is known as Prakrita. If the Prana is restrained by the threefold means of throwing out, taking in and stopping the breath in accordance with the rules prescribed in the Shastras, it is called Vaikrita or artificial, But with great men who have risen above these two kinds of restraining breath, the sudden restraining of the vital currents directly (without inspiration and expiration), is Kevala Kumbhak. Prakrita Pranayam belongs to Mantra Yoga. Vaikrita belongs to Laya Yoga.

35. " That is called Kumbhak (cessation of breath) when there is neither expiration nor inspiration and the body is motionless, remaining still in one state. Then he sees forms like the blind, hears sounds like the deaf and sees the body like wood. This is the characteristic of one who has attained quiescence."

36. Patanjali does not lay much stress on the practice of different kinds of Pranayam. He mentions : " Exhale slowly, then inhale and retain the breath. You will get a steady and calm mind," It is

only the Hatha Yogis who developed Pranayam as a science have mentioned various exercises to suit different persons.

37. "Spread a tiger-skin or a deer-skin or a four-fold blanket. Over this spread a piece of white cloth. Then sit for the Pranayam practice facing the North."

38. Some would take the order as exhaling, inhaling and retaining; others as inhaling, retaining and exhaling. The latter is more common. In Yajnavalkhya, we find the different kinds of breath regulation mentioned in the order of Purak, Kumbhak and Rechak; whereas in Naradiya text we have them in the order as Rechak, Purak, and Kumbhak. The two are to be regulated as optional alternatives.

39. "A Yogi should always avoid fear, anger, laziness, too much sleep or waking and too much food or fasting. If the above rule be well and strictly practised each day, spiritual wisdom will arise of itself in three months without doubt; in four months, he sees the

Devas; in five months he knows or becomes a Brahmanishta; and truly in six months he attains Kaivalya at will. There is no doubt.

40. A neophyte should do Purak and Rechak only without any Kumbhak for some days. Take a long time to do Rechak. The proportion for Purak and Rechak is 1: 2.

41. "Pranayam in its popular and preparatory form may be practised by every one in any posture whatsoever, sitting or walking; and yet it is sure to show its benefits. But to those who practise it in accordance with the specific methods prescribed, fructification will be rapid."

42. Gradually increase the period of Kumbhak. Retain for 4 seconds in the first week, for 8 seconds in the second week, for 12 seconds in the third week and so on till you are able to retain the breath to your full capacity.

43. Commonsense or Yukti should be used throughout your practice. If one kind of exercise is not agreeable to

your system, change it after due consideration or consultation with your Guru. This is Yukti. Where there is Yukti, there is Siddhi, Bhukti and Mukti (enjoyment, perfection and salvation).

44. You must so nicely adjust the Purak, Kumbhak and Rechak that you should not experience the feeling of suffocation or discomfort at any stage of Pranayam. You should never feel the necessity of catching hold of a few normal breaths between any two successive rounds. The duration of Purak, Kumbhak and Rechak must be properly adjusted. Exercise due care and attention. Matters will turn out to be successful and easy.

45. You must not unnecessarily prolong the period of exhalation. If you prolong the time of Rechak, the following inhalation will be done in hurried manner and the rhythm will be disturbed. You must so carefully regulate the Purak, Kumbhak and Rechak that you must be able to be with absolute comfort and care not only of one Pranayam but also

the full course or required rounds of Pranayam. I have to repeat this often. Experience and practice will make you alright. Practice makes one perfect. Be steady. Another important factor is that you must have efficient control over the lungs at the end of Kumbhak to enable you to do the Rechak smoothly and in proportion with the Purak.

46. Suryabheda and Ujjayi produce heat. Sitkari and Sitali are cooling. Bhastrika preserves normal temperature. Suryabheda destroys the excess of wind; Ujjayi phlegm; Sitkari and Sitali bile; and Bhastrika all the three.

47. Suryabheda and Ujjayi must be practised during winter. Sitkari and Sitali must be practised in summer. Bhastrika can be practised in all seasons. Those persons whose bodies are hot even in winter can practise Sitali and Sitkari during winter season.

48. Goal of life is Self-realisation. "This is brought about by means of the subjugation of the body and the senses, the service to a good Guru, the hearing

of Vedantic doctrines and constant meditation thereon" (Niralamba Upa.). If you are really sincere and if you wish to have a quick, sure success, you must have a systematic routine for Asan, Pranayam, Japa, Meditation, Swadhyaya, etc. You must be very careful in keeping up your Brahmacharya. "Effective means to control the mind are the attainment of spiritual knowledge, association with the wise, the entire abdication of all Vasanas and control of Prana" (Muktikopanishad).

49. Once again I wsll tell you that Asan, Pranayam, Japa, Dhyan, Brahmavichar, Sat-sang, Solitude, Mowna, Nishkamya Karma are all absolutely necessary for spiritual attainments. One can hardly obtain perfection in Raja Yoga without Hatha Yoga. At the end of Kumbhak you should withdraw the mind from all the objects. By gradual practice you will be established in Raja Yoga.

50. Some students who are studying Vedantic books think that they are Jnanis and they ignore Asan, Pranayam etc. They also should practise these, till

they are perfect in Shat Sampat of the Sadhan Chatushtaya—Sama, Dama, etc., the preliminary qualifications of Jnana Yoga.

51. Do not hesitate. Do not be waiting to get a Guru who will sit by your side and watch you daily for a long time. If you are sincere, regular and systematic and if you follow the rules and instructions of this book very carefully, there will be no trouble at all. You will undoubtedly get success. Slight errors may crop up in the beginning, It does not matter. Do not unnecessarily be alarmed. Do not give up practice. You will learn yourself how to adjust. Common-sense, instinct, shrill inner voice of the soul will help you in the path. Everything will come out smoothly in the end. Start the practice this very second in right earnest and become a real Yogi.

Om Santi! Santi!! Santi!!!

APPENDIX

APPENDIX

Concentration on Solar Plexus

Solar plexus in often called the abdominal brain. It is an important centre of the nerves, connected with the sympathetic nervous system. It is located in the Epigastric region, behind the pit of the stomach on either side of the spinal column. It has control of the main internal organs of man. It plays a much more important part than is generally recognised. It takes an important part in the control of emotions and of various bodily functions. It is composed of white and gray brain matter. It is one of the most vital parts of the body. A blow over the solar plexus is well-known to boxing-men as a ready means of rendering an opponent unconscious or at any rate helpless. It is the store-house of Prana. It is power-house. It is the most important of all the *Adharas* (support) of the body that are sixteen in number. It is a known fact that men have been instantly killed by a severe blow over the solar plexus. The solar plexus is literally the sun of the nervous system. When this sun is shining harmoniously, the whole of the physical system is harmonious. It radiates strength and energy to all parts of the body. Thoughts and Prana, when directed towards the centre through Pranayam, will stimulate and awaken the sunshine latent therein.

Sit erect in Padmasan or Siddhasan. Close your eyes. Draw the air slowly through the left nostril, as long as you can do with comfort. Keep the right one closed with your right thumb. Repeat OM mentally. Then retain the breath. Have the attention well directed towards the solar plexus. Concentrate your mind there. Have the thought centred upon it. Do not make any undue strain of the mind or undue effort of and kind. Direct consciously the Prana to the region of solar plexus through the retained breath. Imagine: "I am breathing in

Prana, happiness, joy, strength, vigour, love." Then slowly exhale through the right nostril. Then inhale through the right nostril, retain it as before and exhale through the left. Repeat the process 12 times in the morning. Fear, depression, weakness and other undesirable emotions, which stand in the way of spiritual advancement, will vanish. You will become more and more confident of success in Self-realisation.

Pancha Dharana

PRITHVI DHARANA

There are five elements *viz.*, Prithvi, Apas, Agni, Vayu and Akas. To the body of the five elements, there is the five-fold Dharana. From the feet to the knees is said to be the region of the Prithvi. It is four-sided in shape, yellow in colour and has its Varna the Sanskrit letter '*La*' along the region of earth, *i.e.* from the feet to the knees. Contemplating upon this, one should perform Dharana there for a period of two hours daily. He then attains mastery over the earth. Death does not trouble him since he has obtained mastery over the 'earth' element.

AMBASI DHARANA

The region of Apas is said to extend from the knees to the anus. Apas is semilunar in shape and white in colour. It has the letter '*Va*' for its Bijakshara, seed-letter. Carrying up the breath with the letter '*Va*' along the region of Apas, one should contemplate on God Narayan, having four arms, a crowned head, dressed in orange colour clothes and as decayless. Practising Dharana there daily for a period of two hours, he is freed from all sins. Then there is no fear for him from water.

AGNEYI DHARANA

From the anus to the heart is said to be the rgion of Agni. Agni is triangular in shape, red in colour and has the letter '*Ra*' for its Bija. Raising the breath with the letter '*Ra*' along the region of fire, one should contemplate on

Rudra, who has three eyes, who grants all wishes and who is of the colour of midday sun. Practising Dharana there daily for a period of two hours, he is not burnt by fire, even though his body enters into the fire-pit.

VAYU DHARANA

From the heart to the middle of the eye-brows is said to be the region of Vayu. It is black in colour and shines with the letter '*Ya.*' Carrying the breath along the region of Vayu, one should contemplate on Ishwara, the omniscient. The Yogi does not meet his death through Vayu.

AKASI DHARANA

From the centre of the eye-brows to the top of the head is said to be the region of Akas. It is circular in shape, smoky in colour and shines with the letter '*Ha.*' Rising the breath along the region of Akas, one should contemplate on Sadasiva. By practising this Dharana one obtains the power of levitation. The Yogi gets all the Siddhis.

Story of Yogi Bhusunda

Bhusunda is one of the "Chiranjivis" amongst the Yogis. He was the master of the science of Pranayam. It is said that a big nest, like that of a mountain, was built by him on the southern branch of the *Kalpa Vriksha*, situated at the northern summit of the "Mahameru." In this nest, there lived the crow, Bhusunda, by name. This crow, Bhusunda, is said ty be the longest lived Yogi. He was a "*Trikala-Jnani.*" He could cognise all the three periods of time, He could sit in Yoga (Samadhi) for any length of time. He was desireless. He had obtained supreme Santi and Jnana. He was there, enjoying the bliss of his own Self and he is there still, being a Chiranjivi. He was for a long time engaged in the worship of Brahma-shakti "*Aldmbusa.*" At this spot of the Kalpa Vriksha, Bhusunda lived for many Yugas, nay for many Kalpas. He would quit his nest at the time of Pralaya. He had the full knowledge of five Dharanas. He had rendered proof of himself against the five elements, by practising the five methods of concentration. It is said that when all the twelve Adityas scorch the world with their burning rays, he would through his 'Apas Dharana' (water) reach up the Akasa. When the—fierce gabs arise splintering up the rocks to pieces, he would be in the Akasa, through 'Agni Dharana.' When the world together with its Mahameru would be under water, he would float on them without any fluctuation through 'Vayu Dharana,' and when the time of universal destruction arrived, he would be, as in Sushupti, in the Brahmic seat till the beginning of another creation of Brahma. After this creation, he would again resort to the said nest for his abode. The Kalpa Vriksha, at the summit of the mountain, through his Sankalpa (will power) would arise and grow up in the similar way, at the beginning of the next Kalpa every time.

The Inner Factory

The food that you take consists of nitrogenous elements and proteids, fats or hydrocarbons such as ghee and carbohydrates such as rice and sugar. Proteids build up the tissues and the muscles. Carbohydrates produce energy. Besides these, there are various kinds of salts also. The various digestive juices, saliva in the mouth, gastric juice in the stomach, bile, pancreatic juice and the *Succus-entericus* or the intestinal juice in the intestines act upon the particles of food during their passage in the alimentary canal or digestive tube. Saliva acts upon starch. It converts it into sugar. This action is further taken by pancreatic and intestinal juices, in the intestines. Bile acts upon fats. Gastric juice and pancreatic juice act upon proteids. The whole thing is converted into a milky juice called chyle. This chyle is absorbed by lacteal vessels and it is mixed with blood. The right side of the heart contains impure blood. This impure blood is sent to the lungs for purification and after being purified is brought back to the left side of the heart, and from there it is pumped through the big artery aorta, throughout the body. In the capillaries the blood exudes as lymph and bathes and nourishes the tissues and cells of the body, and the impure blood is carried back by veins to the right side of the heart.

The waste products of food are carried along the large intestines which is six feet in length to the rectum where it is retained as faecal matter. When the nervous impulse is carried to the rectum from the defaecation centre in the spinal cord, it is discharged in the morning through the anus, the terminal opening of the alimentary canal.

The kidneys, that are situated in the loins, one on each side eliminate the urine from the blood and send it through two tubes called the ureters to the reservoir of urine called 'bladder.' From the bladder it is discharged through the urethra.

The nervous system consists of cerebrum or forebrain, cerebellum or hind-brain, spinal cord and the sympathetic nerves. There are various centres in the brain for hearing, seeing, tasting, smelling, speaking etc. The efferent impulses from the hands when a finger is stung by a scorpion, are carried through the sensory nerves to the spinal cord and from the spinal cord to the brain. Mind that has taken its seat in the brain, reacts. It feels. An impulse travels from the spinal cord and thence along the motor nerves to the hand. At once the hand is taken back from the scorpion. This all is done in the twinkling of an eye. The sympathetic nerves supply the internal organs, of the abdomen, liver, spleen, heart, etc.

Now I will describe, how this vital fluid semen is manufactured. The two testes or seeds that are located in the scrotal bag are called secretary glands. These cells of the testes have been endowed with the peculiar property of secreting semen drop by drop from the blood, just as the bees collect honey in the honeycomb. Then this fluid is taken by the two spermatic ducts or tubes, two small bags called Vesiculae Seminalis (seminal bags), one on each side of the reservoirs. Under excitement, it is thrown out by small ducts called ejaculatory ducts into the prostatic portion of urethra or urinary canal, where it is mixed with the prostatic juice, secreted by the prostrate gland. Who is the real Director of these internal organs? Who has created this subtle, internal, magnanimous machinery? Are you not struck with awe and wonder, my dear friends, when you think for a moment seriously about the Divine Grandeur and Divine Glory, that is exhibited in the structure of these miraculous mechanisms, heart, lungs, brain etc.? How harmoniously do they work! Who converts food into blood? Who pumps the blood into the arteries? It is He. Feel His Indwelling Presence. Pay Your silent homage to Him. Glory, Glory, unto the Lord, the Creator of this wonderful body, His own image, His own dwelling house, the Navadwarapuri, the ninegated city!

Yogic Diet

A diet that is conducive to the practice of Yoga and spiritual progress can be rightly termed "YOGIC DIET." Diet has intimate connection with the mind. The mind is formed out of the subtlest portion of food. Sage Uddalaka insiructs his son Svetaketu as follows: "Food when consumed becomes threefold, the gross particles become excreta, the middling ones flesh, and the fine ones the mind." Again you will find in the Chandogya Upanishad: "By the purity of food one becomes purified in his nature; by the purification of his nature he verily gets memory of the Self, and by the attainment of memory of the Self, all ties and attachments are severed."

Diet is of three kinds *viz.*, Sattwic diet, Rajasic diet and Tamasic diet. Milk, fruits, cereals, butter, cheese, *tomatoes, spinach* are Sattwic food-stuffs. They render the mind pure. Fish, eggs, meat, etc., are Rajasic food-stuffs. They excite the passion nature of man. Beef, onions, garlic, etc., are Tamasic food-stuffs. They fill the mind with inertia and anger. Lord Krishna says to Arjuna in Gita: "The food which is dear to each is three-fold. Hear thou the distinction of these. The foods which increase vitality, energy, vigour, health, joy and which are delicious, bland, substantial and agreeable are dear to the pure. The passionate man desires foods that are bitter sour, saline, excessively hot, pungent, dry and burning and which produce pain, grief and disease. The food which is stale, tasteless, putrid, rotten and impure is dear to the Tamasic."

[Gita Chap. XVIII—8-10].

Food is of four kinds. There are liquids which are drunk; solids which are pulverized by the teeth and eaten; some solids which are taken in by licking; and soft articles that are swallowed without mastication. All articles of food should be thoroughly masticated in the mouth. Then only they can be readily digested, easily absorbed and assimilated in the system.

The diet should be such as can maintain physical efficiency and good health. The well-being of a man depends or perfect nutrition than on anything else. Various sorts of intestinal diseases, increased susceptibility to infectious diseases, lack of high vitality and power of resistance, rickets, scurvy, anaemia or poverty of blood, beriberi, etc., are all due to faulty nutrition. It should be remembered that it is not so much the climate as food which plays a vital part in producing a strong healthy man or a weakling suffering from a host of diseases. A knowledge of the science of dietetics is essential for every man if he wants to keep up physical efficiency and good health. He should be able to make out a cheap, well-balanced diet from certain articles of diet. Then only all the members of his family will be hale and hearty. What is wanted is a well-balanced diet but not a rich one. A rich diet produces diseases of the liver, kidney, pancreas. A well-balanced diet helps a man to grow, and to turn out much work; increases his body weight and keeps up the efficiency and a high standard of vigour and vitality. A man is what he eats. This is a truism indeed.

Food is required for two purposes. (1) To maintain our body-heat and (2) to produce new cells and to make up for the wear and tear of our bodies. Food-stuffs contain proteins, carbo-hydrates, hydrocarbons, phosphates, salt, various kinds of ashes, water, vitamins, etc. Protein substances are nitrogeneous. They build the tissues of the body. They are present in abundance in dhall, milk, etc. They are called "tissue-builders." Proteins are complex organic compounds which contain carbon, hydrogen, oxygen and nitrogen and sometimes sulphur, phosphorous and iron. Starches are carbo-hydrates. They are present in abundance in rice. Carbo-hydrates are "energy-producers" or heat-givers. Carbo-hydrates are substances like starch, sugar or gum and contain carbon, hydrogen and oxygen. Hydrocarbons or fats are present in ghee and vegetable-oils. Fats are compounds of glycerine with fatty acids. The human machine of the body necessarily needs lubrication. Butter, cream, cheese, groundnut oil, mustard oil, olive oil are good for lubrication.

A well-balanced diet is one in which the different principles of diet that go to keep the body and mind in perfect health and harmony exist in proper proportions. Milk is a perfect food, because it contains all nutritious principles in proper well-balanced proportions. The protein, fat and carbohydrate should be in right proportion. They should be of the right kind also. If a diet contains too much of one thing or too little of another, if it is faulty in one way or the other by being deficient or preponderating in one or more important constituents of food, then it is called an ill-balanced or faulty diet. This will lead to mal-nutrition, stunted growth, physical deficiency, etc. Many diseases take their origin from mal-nutrition. If the food is nutritious, wholesome and well-balanced, one has good power of endurance and physical efficiency. If he has physical efficiency he can turn out more work. Some take milk as an animal diet, while some others regard egg as vegetable-diet. All these people are under a delusion. Milk is a vegetable-diet, while egg is an animal diet. This is the emphatic declaration of learned sages. Yogic students should give up eggs. All the nutritive principles are found in milk, butter, cheese, fruits, almonds tomatoes, carrots and turnips.

The important digestive juices are saliva in the mouth, gastric juice in the stomach, pancreatic juice, bile and intestinal juice(*succus entericus*) in the small intestines. Saliva is alkaline. It is secreted by the salivary glands. It digests starches. Gastric juice is acidic in reaction. It contains Hydrochloric acid. It is secreted by the gastric glands. It digests proteins. Pancreatic juice digests starches, proteins and facts. It contains three kinds of digestive ferments. It is manufactured by the pancreas. Bile is secreted by the liver. It digests fats. The food stuffs are rendered into chyle by the action of these digestive juices, which is absorbed by the lacteals of the small intestines.

Gluttons and epicureans cannot dream to get success in Yoga. He who takes moderate diet, he who has regulated his diet can become a Yogi. That is the reason why Lord Krishna says to Arjuna: "Verily Yoga is not for him who eateth too much, nor who abstaineth to excess nor who is too much addicated to sleep, nor even to wakefulness," Arjuna. "Yoga killeth out all pain for him who is regulated in eating and amusement, regulated in performing actions, regulated in sleeping and waking" (Ch. VI—16, 17). Take pleasent, wholesome and sweet food half-stomachful; fill the quarter stomach with pure water and allow the remaining quarter free for expansion of gas. This is moderate diet.

All articles that are putrid, stale, decomposed, fermented, unclean, twice cooked, kept over-night should be abandoned. The diet should be simple, light, bland, wholesome, easily digestible and nutritious. He who lives to eat is a sinner but he who eats to live is a saint. The latter should be adored. If there is hunger, food can be digested well. If you have no appetite do not take anything, give rest to the stomach.

A good quantity of food overworks the stomach, induces capricious appetite and renders the tongue fastidious. Then it becomes very difficult to please the tongue. Man has invented many kinds of dishes just to satisfy his palate and has made his life very complex and miserable. He calls himself a civilised and cultured man when he is really ignorant and deluded by the senses. His mind gets upset when he cannot get his usual dishes in a new place. Is this real strength? He has become an absolute slave of his tongue. This is bad. Be natural and simple in eating.

Eat to live and do not live to eat You can be really happy and can devote much time to Yogic practices.

A Yogic student who spends his time in pure meditation only, wants very little food. One or one and a half seer of milk and some fruits suffice. But when he comes on the platform for work he wants abundant nutritious food. A man who does immense labour (physical work) wants more food.

Meat is not at all necessary for the keeping up of health. Meat-eating is highly deleterious to health. It brings host of ailments such as tape-worm, albuminuria and other diseases of the kidneys. After all man wants very little on this earth. Killing of animals for food is a great sin. Instead of killing the egoism and the idea of "mine-ness" ignorant people kill innocent animals under the pretext of sacrifice to Goddess but it is really to satisfy their tongues and palates. Horrible! Most inhuman! "*Ahimsa Paramo Dharma.* Ahimsa is the first virtue that a spiritual aspirant should possess." We should have reverence for life. Lord Jesus says: "Blessed are the merciful, for they shall obtain mercy." Lord Jesus and Mahavir shouted at the top of their voice: "Regard every living being as thyself and harm no one." The law of Karma is inexorable unrelenting and immutable. The pain you inflict upon another will rebound upon you and the happiness you radiate to another will come back to you, adding to your happiness.

Dr. J. Oldfield, Senior physician, Lady Margaret Hospital, writes: "To-day, there is the chemical fact in the hands of all, which none can gainsay that the products of the vegetable kingdom contain all that is necessary for the fullest sustenance of human life. Flesh is unnatural food, and therefore, tends to create functional disturbances. As it is taken in modern civilisation, it is infected with such terrible diseases (readily transferable to man), as cancer, consumption, fever, intestinal worms, etc., to an enormous extent. There is little need for wonder that flesh eating is one of the most serious causes of the diseases that carry off ninety-nine out of every hundred people that are born."

Meat eating and alcoholism are closely allied. The craving for liquor dies a natural death when the meat diet is withdrawn. The question of birth-control becomes very difficult in the case of those who take meat diet. To them mind control is absolutely impossible. Mark how the meat-eating tiger is ferocious, and the cow, elephant, which live on grass are mild and peaceful! Meat has a direct evil influence on the compartments of the brain. The first step in the spiritual advancement is the giving up of meat diet. The divine light will not descend if the stomach is loaded with meat diet. In large meat-eating countries cancer mortality is very high. Vegetarians keep up sound health till old age. Even in the West in the Hospitals, doctors are now putting patients on vegetable diet. They convalesce very quickly.

Pythagoras, the Grecian Sage, condemned meat diet as sinful food! Just hear what he says: "Beware O mortals, of defiling you bodies with sinful food! There are cereals, there are fruits, bending their branches down by their weight, and luxurious grapes on the vines. There are sweet vegetables and herbs, which the flame can render palatable and mellow. Nor are you denied milk, nor fragrance of the aroma of the thyma flower, The bountiful earth offers you an abundance of pure food and provides for meals obtainable without slaughter and bloodshed."

If you want to stop taking mutton, fish, etc., just see with your own eyes the pitiable, struggling condition at the time of killing the sheep. Now mercy and sympathy will arise in your heart. Then you will determine to give up flesh eating. If you fail in this attempt, just change your environments and live in a vegetarian hotel where you cannot get mutton and fish. Move in that society where there is only vegetable diet. Always think of the evils of flesh eating and the benefits of a vegetable diet. If this also cannot give you sufficient strength to stop this habit, go to the slaughter house and butcher's shop and personally see the disgusting rotten muscles, intestines, kidneys and other nasty parts of the animal which emit bad smell. This will induce Vairag in you and a strong disgust and hatred for meat-eating.

It is not only a heinous but an atrocious crime to kill a cow or a goat which gives invaluable milk, butter, etc. O Self-deluded ignorant cruel man! do not kill these innocent beings. Terrible torture awaits you on the day of judgment. You are morally responsible for all your acts. The law of Karma is infallible. Killing of cows tantamounts to killing one's own mother. What right have you got to take away the lives of these innocent animals which give you milk to nourish your body? This is a most brutal, inhuman, heart-rending act. The slaughter of cows, goats and other animals should be immediately stopped by legislation. The animal that is taken for slaughter throws various sorts of poisons in the blood on account of fear, anger. The vegetarian diet can fully supply the dietetic needs of the body. Therefore such cruelties are unwarranted.

I shall speak a word now on vitamins. Vitamins are also required in the diet. They build the bodies. If they are absent or deficient, the body cannot grow, and deficiency diseases such as rickets, scurvy result. They are present in very small quantities in foods. They are like a spark which ignites the fire of nutrition. There are four important kinds of vitamins:—Vitamin A, Vitamin B, Vitamin C. and Vitamin D. Vitamin A is present in milk. Vitamin B is present in the unpolished rice and tomato juice. Deficiency of Vitamin B causes beriberi. Those who eat polished rice get this disease. Vitamin C is found in vegetables, fruits and green leaves. This vitamin is destroyed by cooking, tinning. Sailors suffer from scurvy, because they cannot get fresh vegetables and fruits during long voyage. They generally take with them the juice of lemons. This prevents the development of scurvy. Vitamin D is present in milk, butter, eggs, cod-liver oil, etc. Absence or deficiency of vitamin D causes rickets in children.

Food is nothing but a mass of energy, Food supplies energy to the body and mind. If you can draw this energy from your pure will. if you know the Yogic technique of absorbing the energy directly from the sun or cosmic Prana, you can maintain the body with this energy and can dispense with food altogether. The Yogi gets Kayasidhi or perfection of the body.

If food is completely digestible it will produce constipation. Food should contain some residue of fibres or husks which will form faecal matter. No water should be taken when digestion is going on in the stomach. It will dilute the digestive juice and impair digestion. You can take a glassful of water when you have finished your meals,

Where can Sannyasins who live on public alms get a well-balanced diet? They get some days pungent stuffs only, on some other days sweetmeats only, on some other days sour things only. But they draw the required energy through the power of meditation. This unique, Yogic method is unknown to the medical profession and to the scientists. Whenever the mind is concentrated, a divine wave bathes all the tissues with the divine elixir. All the cells are renovated and vivified.

Fasting is interdicted for practitioners of Yoga as it produces weakness. Occasional mild fast is highly beneficial. It will thoroughly overhaul the system, will give rest to the stomach and intestines and eliminate uric acid. Yogic students can take one full meal at 11 o'clock a cup of milk in the morning and half a seer of milk and 2 bananas or 2 oranges or 2 apples at night. The night meals should be very light. If the stomach is loaded, sleep will supervene. A diet consisting of milk and fruits alone is a splendid menu for students of Yoga.

Simple, natural, non-stimulating, tissue-building, energy-producing, non-alcoholic foods and drinks keep the mind calm and pure and help the Yogic practices and in the attainment of the goal of life.

DINACHARYA

ELEMENTARY COURSE "A" FOR BUSY PEOPLE

	H. M.	From		To
Sirshasan ...	0—5			
Sarvangasan ...	0—5			
Matsyasan ...	0—3	4—0	A.M.	4-25
Paschimottanasan ...	0—5			
Other Asanas ...	0—5			
Savasan ...	0—2			
Rest ...	0—5	4-25	„	4-30
Bhastrika ...	0—5	4-30	„	4-40
Other Pranayams ...	0—5			
Japa and Meditation ...	0-50	4-40	„	5-30
Study ...	0-30	5-30	„	6—0
Physical exercises and/or walking	1—0	6—0	„	7—0
Asan, Pranayam, Japa and Meditation	1-30	6-15	P.M.	7-45
Bhajan (Kirtan) ...	0-30	7-45	„	8-15
Meals and Rest ...	0-15	8-15	„	8-30
Study ...	1—0	8-30	„	9-30
Sleep ...	6—0	9-30	„	3-30

ADVANCED COURSE "B" FOR BUSY PEOPLE

	H. M.	From		To
Meditation ...	1—0	3-30	A.M.	4-30
Sirshasan ...	0-30	4-30	„	5—0

	H. M.	From		To
Sarvangasan, Paschimottan, Mayurasan and other Asanas ...	0-30	5—0	A.M.	5-30
Bhastrika and/or other Pranayams ...	0-30	5-30	„	6—0
Japa ...	0-30	6—0	„	6-30
Study ...	0-30	6-30	„	7—0
Asan, Pranayam, Japa and Meditation ...	3—0	6-15	P.M.	9-15
Meals ...	0-15	9-15	„	9-30
Study ...	0-30	9-30	„	10-0
Sleep ...	5—0	10-0	„	3—0

COMMON ROUTINE FOR "A" AND "B" COURSES

	H. M.	From		To
Rest, Chota Hazri or a cup of milk ...	0-15	7—0	A.M.	7-15
Nishkamya Karma and household duties ...	1-15	7-15	„	8-30
Bathing, washing, breakfast, etc. ...	1—0	8-30	„	9-30
Office ...	3—0	10-0	„	1—0
Lunch, writing letters and interview ...	1—0	1—0	P.M.	2—0
Office ...	3—0	2—0	„	5—0
Evening tiffin and rest ...	0-15	5—0	„	5-15
Evening walk 2 miles Satsang, Sravana ...	1—0	5-15	„	6-15

COURSE "C" FOR WHOLE-TIMED ASPIRANTS

Meditation	...	3—0	3-30	A.M.	6-30
Asan, Pranayam	...	2—0	6-30	„	8-30
Japa	...	0-30	8-30	„	9—0
Asan, Pranayam	...	2—0	5—0	P.M.	7—0
Bhajan and Japa	...	0-30	7—0	„	7-30
Meditation	...	2-30	7-30	„	10-0
Sleep	...	5—0	10-0	„	3—0

During other times Mowna, Nishkamya Karma. Kirtan, study, bath, meals, rest, etc., must be nicely arranged. The aspirants should have their own routine according to their growth, capacity and convenience.

Important Hints

1. Every aspirant in Yoga should have a similar routine. You can make a few changes in time here and there; but every item of the routine should be there. Mere Vedantic gossipping will not do in the spiritual path. You must be very strict in observing punctuality and every item of the routine should be carried out at any cost. The time given for meditation, Japa, Asan and Pranayam should be gradually increased.

2. As soon as you get up from bed, evacuate you bowels first; wash your hands, legs, head and face if you cannot take a bath; and then sit for meditation and other Yogic practices.

3. After regular practice for some days, if you increase the period of doing Asan, Pranayam and meditation, you will have to curtail the item that is allotted to household duties and morning walk. On holidays more time should be utilized for spiritual practices.

4. During the period of the morning 'study', you should read Gita, Upanishads, Ramayan, etc., and in the night study you can read some other philosophical books or journals. These two items are something like the detailed and non-detailed texts of the students. You can utilize the time of interview and writing letters in studying some interesting books.

5. During evening walk, you can profitably combine other physical exercises and a few rounds of Pranayam. While you practise Pranayam and during other work also, mentally do Japa.

6. When you perform Kirtan in the night, include your family, children and servants also. In the end distribute Prasad.

7. Under the heading Nishkamya Karma, treatment or nursing of the sick is the best. If you cannot do this, give private tuition for the poor students or distribute charity.

8. Due to unavoidable circumstances if you cannot attend to any item of the routine, that time should be utilized for Mowna, study or gardening. The mind must be kept busy always in doing similar useful work.

9. In the short course "A," Asan, Pranayam can be done first and then Japa and Meditation. In the advanced course "B," Asan, Pranayam should be practised after Japa and Meditation, as the morning time 'Brahma Muhurta' is the best for meditation. To drive away drowsiness, you can practise Sirshasan or Bhastrika for about 10 minutes, before starting Japa and Meditation.

10. If you fail to do any one of the items, dear brother, please note that you have killed a day in your precious life. In case you find any disturbing elements in the world, mercilessly without any hesitation renounce the world and take to seclusion and devote day and night for spiritual Sadhan at the Lotus Feet of your Guru. If you are steady, earnest and sincere, in six months time you will find an inexpressible joy, mental peace and unalloyed bliss. There will be Jyoti in your very face. Such a man is really a blessing for the whole world. This kind of Sadhan alone can give you eternal satisfaction and happiness. You will have to repent in your old age if you depend for your happiness on a few ginger biscuits, little money and a woman.

Om Santi! Santi!! Santi!!!

Hari Om Tat Sat.

QUESTIONS and ANSWERS

Q. Is it right to say that Pranayama is unnecessary in the practice of Raja Yoga.

A. No; Pranayama forms one of the eight limbs of Raja Yoga.

Q. Is it dangerous to practise Pranayama without the assistance of a Guru (Teacher)?

A. People are unnecessarily alarmad. You can practise ordinary Pranayama exercises without the help of a Guru. A Guru is necessary if you want to practise Kumbhaka or retention of breath for a long time and unite Apana with Prana. The books written by realised Yogins can guide you if you are not able to get a Guru. But it is better to have a Guru by your side or you can get the lessons from him and practise them at home. You can keep regular correspondence with him. You can retain the breath from ½ to 1 or 2 minutes without any difficulty or danger. If you cannot get a realised Yogi, you can approach senior students of Yoga. They also can help you.

Q. Will the practice of Pranayama alone awaken the sleeping Kundalini Shakti?

A. No. Asan, Bandhas, Mudras, Pranayama, Japa, Meditation, strong and pure irresistible analytical will, the grace of a Guru, devotion,—all these will awaken the Kundalini Shakti.

Q. What are the effects of the practice of Kechari Mudra?

A. It will help the student to stop the breath. He can have nice concentration and meditation. He will be free from hunger and thirst. He can change the breath from one nostril to another quite easily. He can have Kevala Kumbhaka also very easily.

Q. What are the symptoms when Prana and Apana are united and when the Prana passes in Sushumna?

A. When Prana and Apana is united, the united Prana-Apana will pass through the Sushumna and the practitioner will become dead to the world i.e., he will lose the consciousness of his body, environments and the world but will have perfect awareness. He will feel Divine Thrill, Divine Ecstacy and the experiences of the lower stages of Samadhi. When the Prana proceeds higher in Sushumna, different kind of experiences at different Chakras are experienced by the practitioner (which cannot be described, but should be experiened). When the Prana reaches Sahasrar, the Yogi attains Samadhi.

Q. Should one during the practice of Pranayama during Maha Bandha also maintain the proportion 1:4:2?

A. Yes; in Maha Bandha the proportion for inhalation, retention and expiration is 1:4:2.

Q. If one practises Bandha Traya Pranayama and suppose he practises Puraka 10 Matras, Kumbhaka 40 Matras and relaxation 20 Matras how long must be the pure Kumbhaka and how long the expiratory pause with Uddiyana?

A. In Bandha Traya, beginners need not have any expiratory pause. Advanced students can have it for 5 or 6 seconds. In Bandha Traya, the main Kumbhak (1 : 4 : 2) is quite sufficient for the Union of Prana Apana.

Q. What is the difference between Tadan Kriya and Maha Vedha?

A. In Tadan Kriya one can breathe in in any way. But in Maha Vedha Pranayama should be practised as described in Bandha Traya.

Q. Is Pranayama necessary for getting Darshan of the Lord?

A. No.

Q. When the Prana is taken up to the tenth door, (Brahmarandhra) on the crown of the head, will the practitioner feel a pinprick?

A. No.

Q. What is Oordhwareta Pranayama?

A. While doing Sukh Purvak or Loma-Viloma Pranayama feel that the Veerya is flowing up towards the Sahasrara at the crown of the head in the form of Ojas. This is Oordhwareta Pranayama.

Q. If I try to keep up the ratio 1:4:2 when I practise Pranayama I am not able to concentrate on my Ishta Devata. If I try to concentrate, I cannot keep up the ratio 1:4:2. Kindly advise what to do?

A. Try to keep the ratio for two or three months. A strong habit will be formed and the ratio will be kept up automatically. Then you can concentrate on your tutelary diety. Mind can do only one thing at a time.

Q. What is the object of inhaling through the left nostril and exhaling through the left and vice versa?

A. This will make the breath rhythmical, steady the nerves and the mind and allow the Sushumna Nadi to flow which will be beneficial for meditation. It will keep up a perfect harmony in the system. The five Koshas will vibrate rhythmically.

Q. Can there be any dangerous results in the practice of Pranayama as some people think?

A. There is no danger in practising Pranayama, Asans etc., if you are careful, if you use your common sense. People are unnessarily alarmed. There is danger in everything, if you are careless.

If you are careless in getting down through the steps of a staircase, you will fall down and break your bones. If you are careless when you walk in the busy parts of a city, you will be crushed by the motor car. If you are careless when you purchase a ticket at the Railway Station, you will lose your money-purse. If you are careless in dispensing mixtures you will kill the patients by giving a poison or a wrong medicine or administering a medicine in over-doses. Even so, when you practise Pranayama and other Yogic exercises you will have to be careful about your diet. You should avoid over-loading; you should take light, easily digestible and nutritious food. You should not go beyond your capacity in retaining the breath. You should first practise inhalation and exhalation only (without retention of breath) for one or two months. You should gradually increase the ratio from 1: 4: 2 to 16: 64: 32. You should exhale very very slowly. If these rules are observed, there will be no danger at all in the practice of Pranayam and other Yogic exercises.

Printed at the Vaman Press, 31, Broadway, Madras.

